THE SELF-POSSESSED SHIELD

*How to Set Luxury Boundaries,
Exude Feminine Energy &
The Confidence That Protects Your Peace*

Kele Chi Key

© 2025 Key Noble Quill LLC
All rights reserved.

No part of this book may be reproduced, distributed, transmitted, or stored in any form or by any means, including photocopying, recording, or other electronic or mechanical methods, without the prior written permission of the publisher, except in the case of brief quotations embodied in critical reviews and certain other noncommercial uses permitted by copyright law.

ISBN: 979-8-9943245-0-9
Published by Key Noble Quill LLC

Acknowledgments

I would like to thank God for the renewal of my mind and the clarity that transformed the way I see myself, my life, and my purpose.

Through Him, I was given the wisdom to question learned ideologies and beliefs shaped by culture and upbringing—especially those that required self-sacrifice at the expense of well-being. He gave me the will, the strength, and the discernment to make necessary changes, even when they were uncomfortable or misunderstood.

I am grateful for the confidence He placed in me to live differently, to choose myself with intention, and to share what I have learned in the hope that it encourages and empowers other women to do the same.

When I found God, my life began to make sense. With that clarity came alignment, purpose, and the courage to stand firmly in who I am becoming. This work is possible because of that foundation.

Dedication

This book is dedicated to the women who have given endlessly to family, to work, to relationships, to expectations while quietly placing themselves last. To the women who kept going, kept showing up, and kept their promises to everyone else, even when doing so cost them their energy, their peace, and sometimes their joy.

This is an invitation to come back to yourself. It is a reminder that taking charge of your life is not selfish, it is necessary. That releasing unnecessary stress, emotional weight, and unspoken burdens is an act of love, not neglect. That choosing yourself is one of the most responsible decisions you will ever make.

This book is for the woman learning how to be her best self not by doing more, but by honoring herself more. By loving herself deeply enough to remove what disrupts her peace, drains her spirit, or asks her to abandon her well-being. It is for the woman who chooses to exude femininity with intention, grace, and inner strength and who understands that being labeled difficult, selective, or misunderstood is sometimes the price of protecting her health, her future, and her sense of self.

This work is also for the woman unlearning inherited beliefs, cultural conditioning, and societal expectations that taught her to overextend, endure silently, or earn rest through sacrifice.

Above all, this book is dedicated to loving ourselves in the highest form so that we may live longer, healthier, more fulfilled lives, and be fully present for the people and purposes that truly deserve our love.

Author's Note

Dear Woman,

This book was written for women who are ready to take responsibility for their lives. For women who understand that well-being, longevity, and fulfillment are built through intention, discernment, and the willingness to be clear about how they expect to be treated. Too often, women are taught to give endlessly, endure quietly, and place themselves last in order to meet cultural or societal expectations. This work exists to challenge that conditioning.

Within these pages, femininity is presented as self-leadership grounded in standards, structure, and self-respect. It includes the ability to be warm and compassionate, as well as the capacity to be firm and assertive when necessary. Boundaries here are not reactions or defenses; they are conscious decisions that protect energy, health, and peace.

This book is not about explaining yourself to gain approval or convincing others of your worth. It is about learning to prioritize yourself, release unnecessary emotional and energetic burdens, and remove people, patterns, and environments that deplete your well-being. Some of what you read may affirm what you already know; other parts may require unlearning beliefs shaped by culture, upbringing, or expectations that reward sacrifice over sustainability.

This book is meant to be read with intention. Take your time with it. Apply what resonates. Sit with what challenges you. The goal is alignment between how you live, what you tolerate, and what you choose to carry forward.

Above all, this work is an invitation to love yourself at the highest level. To live in a way that supports health, longevity, and fulfillment. And to show up fully and intentionally for the people and purposes that truly deserve your time, energy, and care.

How to Read This Book

This book is not meant to be rushed or consumed for motivation alone. It is meant to be engaged with intentionally. You are not required to agree with every page to benefit from the work. Read with discernment. Notice what resonates immediately, and pay equal attention to what challenges you. Discomfort often signals a place where unlearning is necessary.

Some chapters may feel affirming. Others may ask you to examine long-held beliefs shaped by culture, family, or societal expectations, especially those that taught you to overextend, tolerate quietly, or place your needs last. Take your time with these sections. Apply what aligns. Release what no longer serves the woman you are becoming.

This book is designed to support self-leadership, not dependency. You will not find scripts, performances, or instructions on how to be accepted. Instead, you are encouraged to observe your patterns, assess where your energy is going, and make deliberate decisions about what and who you allow access to your life. Read this book in moments when you can be honest with yourself. Pause when necessary. Reflect before moving forward. Growth does not require urgency; it requires clarity and consistency.

Most importantly, allow this book to meet you where you are without pressure to become someone else. The work is not about perfection, performance, or approval. It is about alignment: between how you live, what you tolerate, and the standards you choose to uphold. Return to this book as needed. Its purpose is not to be finished quickly, but to be lived with.

TABLE OF CONTENTS

Acknowledgments	3
Dedication	4
Author's Note	6
Introduction	11
CHAPTER 1	18
The Feminine Energy	18
CHAPTER 2	33
Feeling Good as a Non-Negotiable	33
CHAPTER 3	51
Advocacy Wrapped in Grace	51
CHAPTER 4	70
Refusing to Shrink	70
CHAPTER 5	91
The Concept of Attraction	91
CHAPTER 6	110
The Daily Practice of Walking "Shoulders-high"	110
CHAPTER 7	128
Luxury Is a Behavior, Not a Price Tag	128
CHAPTER 8	149
Prioritizing Yourself	149
CHAPTER 9	167
The Self-possessed Shield in Practice	167

About the Author 188

Introduction

They do not always tell us that being a woman has now mimicked sheer work: struggling to live up to the standards people casually set through stereotypes and patriarchy. Adjusting a lot, always, managing to fit, and, to crown it all, over-explaining why you deserve basic respect.

What they do tell us on the contrary, is to be 'good women'. And the patriarchal definition of good women which we were taught to be, has never been one for our benefit: Kind, accommodating, obedient, self-sacrificing, and agreeable, ambition-limited.

I come from a place that often teaches that a woman's worth is measured in her malleability. You must be gentle enough to bend but strong enough to carry the weight of everyone's expectations. You must be educated but not opinionated, ambitious but not threatening, beautiful but not vain, and independent but not difficult. And somehow, in the margins of all this performing, you need to still remain the woman that you are. They want you feminine. But you must know that femininity here mostly means available, accommodating, and endlessly forgiving. When you set a boundary, suddenly you're proud, you've changed, or what's most popular, "forgotten your home training." When someone disrespects you, still, you must smile and greet them properly the next time you see them. Respect becomes a one-way transaction that only flows upward and outward, never back to you.

How does one woman carry this all?

So, we lose ourselves in the translation between who we are and who we must become to be considered a good woman, culturally. And the tragedy is not just that we disappear, but that we're applauded for it. They call it maturity, wisdom, or knowing your place. But I've watched too many women fold themselves into societal shapes they were never meant to hold, and seen their edges smoothed away until they no longer recognize the face in the mirror. And still, it's never enough.

You must have now noticed the imbalance here. You see, no one teaches a woman how to be a "protected woman" and no one truly explains how we are to do all that, without getting disrespected, drained, or taken for granted. Women are told to be confident, but not how to carry that confidence without becoming hardened or exhausted. Women are told to be feminine, but not taught how to stay feminine whilst still enforcing and maintaining healthy, luxury boundaries, and to do this without feeling guilty, defensive, or aggressive. We downplay our needs, so we don't look "difficult." We endure, because we are taught that endurance is a virtue. And soon, we're waking up one day, feeling tired, resentful, and slightly disconnected from ourselves.

Through many years of observation, analysis, and living it myself, I have come to believe that advice often given to women is either incomplete or placed for leverage. As though these were designed to gain control over women and their choices too. I discovered early that femininity, confidence, and boundaries are meant to work together, and not as three separate personalities a woman has to switch to, depending on the situation. This, because femininity without boundaries gets violated, in the same way confidence without femininity can feel harsh and tiring, and boundaries without confidence can feel shaky and apologetic. When one is missing, the whole system collapses. This system is the window through which the world experiences you.

When I started my career in healthcare as a Nursing student, it became even more obvious. If you know anything about nursing school, you know it's brutally hard. It's stressful, demanding, and emotionally draining. Yet, every day before I left my house, I always ensured that I was well-groomed and properly put together. My classmates used to ask: "How long does it take you to get ready?" And they meant it. Genuinely. I understood that their concerns stemmed mostly from the fact that nursing school was already a chore. But how could basic self-care be viewed as an extra shift I was adding to my day? Their question always confused me, a little more than it should have. For me, the case was this: while I may have been going through a lot at that school, I cared about myself enough to show up as myself. I didn't have to look like what I was going through just to prove I was doing a difficult course. It sounded silly to me.

Later, when I started working as a nurse, people (especially other women), continued to react negatively to this lifestyle of being well put

THE SELF-POSSESSED SHIELD

together. Some others assumed I wasn't competent. For them, I couldn't possibly be serious about my job if I looked too feminine. My patients, on the other hand, loved it. And they didn't only trust me, but also felt safe around me as they had openly declared. This was my first take-home, and it proves that femininity does not weaken you, it only changes how people experience you.

This book brings together the three things that changed my life once I understood how they work together. First, femininity. Not as an aesthetic, but as a frequency. As a lifestyle beyond appearance, learning to trust how things *feel*, and exuding that energy to get the life you deserve. Second, confidence. The kind that comes from self-respect, consistency, and internal standards that you do not negotiate. Third, boundaries. Not walls or aggression, but as a luxury form of protection. The ability to say "no" without explaining yourself to exhaustion and to walk away without drowning in guilt. Together, they form what I think of as a shield.

What this means is that you do not always have to harden or shrink. You simply become a woman who doesn't accept what she doesn't deserve. If you're running from exhaustion of this sheer work of being a woman, this book is a safe place. Society didn't tell you everything, but the woman that I am would. I do not teach becoming hard to survive, disrespect for culture, or some sort of uncoordinated rebellion. The message is that you do not have to choose between being feminine and being respected. You don't have to become cold to stop being taken advantage of. You don't have to apologize for wanting peace, for expecting better, for saying no without a dissertation on why.

This book will show you how to hold all of it: your femininity, your boundaries and your confidence without betraying yourself in the process. How to move through the world as someone kind but not susceptible, kind but not conquered, open but not available to everyone. This book is permission, if you'll see it as one. It is permission to rest from the performance. To stop shrinking and take up space without explaining why you deserve it. If you've been waiting for someone to tell you that you're not too much, not too difficult, not too demanding for wanting to be treated well while staying true to yourself, consider this at that moment.

How can you call yourself broken when you're only just tired from living the norm? You're awake. And that's exactly where transformation begins. If you're ready to stop surviving womanhood and start inhabiting it, let's build your shield together.

CHAPTER 1
The Feminine Energy

There was a certain time when I thought that femininity was something you either leaned into or defended yourself against. Depending on the room you were walking into, or depending on how tired you already were, or even depending on how much resistance you could afford that day. It felt like a switch you flipped on when it was safe and tucked away when it wasn't. I didn't have a language for it then. I only knew the tension.

Growing up, I learnt early that being a woman came with expectations that were never announced properly. They arrived through comments, corrections, raised eyebrows, and praise that always felt conditional. You were allowed to be gentle, but only if it did not inconvenience anyone. Intelligent, but not assertive. Capable, but not confrontational. Beautiful, but never too aware of it. Femininity, as it was handed to us, felt less like a birthright and more like a narrow hallway you had to walk through without brushing the walls.

For a long time, I thought the discomfort meant something was wrong with me. Maybe I was doing womanhood incorrectly. It took years of watching, missteps, and a fair amount of exhaustion to realize that the problem was not femininity itself, but the way it had been reduced to performance. I've come to learn that when something is constantly misunderstood, it gets distorted. And femininity has been misunderstood for a very long time.

How is Femininity Better Defined?

It is safe to say that femininity resists rigid definitions. So, it is best to explore it as something lived rather than explained or performed, because once you understand what feminine energy actually is, the rest of the work begins to make sense.

What I've come to understand is that femininity is not fragile, it's perceptive. And neither is it passive, it's responsive. It notices things before they announce themselves, it reads rooms, and it feels when something is off long before words catch up. This sensitivity is often mocked or dismissed, but I've learned that it is one of the most powerful forms of intelligence a woman carries.

I do not believe men and women are equal in the sense of sameness. Not because one is more important than the other, but because sameness was never the goal. We are designed differently, built with different strengths, different pressures, different responsibilities. A woman will never be a man, and a man will never be a woman. That distinction is not a disadvantage, it is a structure. Balance does not come from erasing differences, it comes from knowing how to stand inside them without apology. Somewhere along the way, difference was mistaken for deficiency. Femininity was treated like something that needed justification, or that had to prove its usefulness before it was allowed to exist. And so women were taught to either lighten it to the point of disappearance or harden themselves to survive without it. Both options came at a cost.

Acknowledging differences does not mean accepting limitations. Understanding that men and women are not the same does not require shrinking yourself, it requires knowing where your power actually lives. For many women, that power is not loud. It does not announce itself. It regulates itself. It chooses its moments carefully. It does not waste energy proving what it already knows. I've watched women confuse emotional composure with emotional suppression. They are not the same. Composure comes from knowing yourself well enough not to react to everything, while suppression comes from fear of consequence. Femininity thrives in the former and withers in the latter. When a woman feels safe within herself, her femininity becomes stable rather than fragile.

Some women often shrink in environments that do not know what to do with their presence. Not because they lack competence, but because they carry themselves in ways that challenge outdated ideas of seriousness and strength. This, I saw most clearly when I started my career in healthcare. I've learned that how a woman presents herself is not separate from her inner world. Aesthetics and energy are in conversation with each other. How you look is often a reflection of what you tolerate, how you regulate yourself, and the standards you uphold. It is not about dressing for approval or performing for comfort. It is about alignment.

THE SELF-POSSESSED SHIELD

When a woman's internal world is settled, her external presentation tends to follow.

Femininity, in its truest sense, is not about submission or silence. It is about presence, about carrying yourself in a way that does not beg to be understood. It's about knowing when to speak and when to step back, not out of fear, but out of self-respect. It is the difference between reacting and responding. It is important to speak up. Don't be cute and mute.

I've also noticed how differently femininity is expressed depending on culture and environment. Women in Nigeria, for instance, often carry a strength that is both warm and formidable. There is resilience there, layered with grace, humor, and endurance. In other places, femininity shows up more reserved and more contained with different expressions and the same essence. What changes is not the energy, but what it is allowed to look like. The trouble actually begins when femininity is mistaken for weakness, or worse, when women are taught to believe that themselves. When femininity is seen as something to exploit rather than something to respect, without self-regulation and standards, that femininity becomes vulnerable in the wrong way. Not open, but exposed and unprotected.

I didn't understand this early on. I only knew that certain spaces drained me more than others. Those certain interactions left me feeling unsettled. Over time, I realized it was because I hadn't yet learned how to carry myself with intention. Femininity is not just something you put on, you have to stabilize it within yourself, it should become the internal frequency that informs how you move, how you choose, and how you allow yourself to be treated. When that frequency is grounded, people respond differently because energy always speaks before words do.

For a long time, I watched conversations about femininity swing wildly between extremes. Either it was romanticized into something ornamental and harmless, or dismissed as outdated and limiting. Both interpretations felt incomplete, and neither reflected the women I knew, and had grown up around, or the woman I was becoming. Femininity, as I experienced it, was far more nuanced than what those arguments allowed.

Clearing The Misconceptions

One of the biggest misunderstandings I've come across is the idea that femininity is passive. That to be feminine is to wait, tolerate, and accept whatever comes your way with a pleasant expression and minimal resistance. I believed this for a while too, or at least I tried to live it. I mistook receptivity for self-abandonment and called it grace. It took me some bruises to learn the difference.

Contrary to beliefs, a receptive woman is not open to everything, she is selective, she senses when something aligns and when it doesn't, and she trusts herself enough to act on that information efficiently. I've come to notice that women are often encouraged to override their inner sensing. We are told not to read too much into things, not to be sensitive, not to make a fuss. Over time, that advice disconnects us from our instincts. We learn to doubt what we feel even when our bodies are responding clearly, and the irony is that this emotional attunement, this ability to feel texture in interactions, is one of the most refined forms of intelligence we possess. I learnt this slowly, mostly through paying attention to how certain rooms made me feel. There were spaces where I walked in and immediately felt smaller, though nothing overt had happened yet. Conversations that left a residue I couldn't explain. People who smiled warmly but carried an undertone of dismissal. At first, I blamed myself for being perceptive. I thought maybe I was imagining things. Over time, patterns emerged. It was the same discomfort and misalignment. I had to learn to trust that signal.

Femininity operates through this awareness. It notices tone shifts, energy changes, what is being said, and what is being avoided. It picks up on when effort is uneven, when respect is conditional, and when interest is performative. This isn't paranoia or insecurity, it's attentiveness. The problem is that attentiveness in women is often reframed as overthinking so that it can be ignored.

Another myth I've had to unlearn is that femininity exists for approval, that it needs an audience, particularly a male one, to be valid. This belief is subtle but pervasive. It shows up in the pressure to be palatable, desirable, and agreeable. It suggests that femininity loses value when it is not being received or praised, and this couldn't be further from the truth.

Femininity is self-referenced. It does not wait to be affirmed before it settles into itself. When a woman is grounded in her standards and at ease with her choices, her energy becomes steady. She is not auditioning, she is not adjusting herself to be easier to digest, she simply exists as she is, and that steadiness becomes unmistakable. This is where a lot of conversations around feminism get tangled. Somewhere along the line, femininity was positioned as something that had to be defended or rejected for a woman to be taken seriously. Strength became synonymous with hardness, and independence was framed as emotional detachment.

I've experienced firsthand how quickly femininity can be misread as incompetence or frivolity. Also, how attractiveness can invite assumptions that have nothing to do with ability. And yet, I've also seen how consistency dismantles those assumptions over time. Femininity does not need to be defended when it is anchored. It speaks for itself eventually. What I've come to believe is that feminine energy is not something you summon. It's something you stop disrupting. When a woman regulates her emotions, honors her boundaries, and lives by internal standards she respects, her energy settles. She becomes harder to rush, harder to pressure, harder to dismiss. I didn't arrive here overnight. I arrived through mistakes, exhaustion, moments where I realized I was giving too much access to people who had not earned it, and each experience refined my understanding.

Femininity, I learnt, is not about enduring everything with grace. It is about knowing what deserves your grace in the first place. And once that distinction becomes clear, everything else begins to reorganize itself. People respond instinctively to presence. It actually took me time to untangle femininity from fragility. I got to learn that it isn't about how you appear, or how well you smile through discomfort, or about who you can accommodate, or how you can be in the face of disrespect.

True femininity is about being aligned internally so that your external presence carries your standards without you needing to explain them. It's about being receptive but not vulnerable to exploitation. It's about emotional awareness without overextending your energy. I've noticed that women often undervalue this because it doesn't fit the popular narrative of "power" or "strength." But in reality, it is the power that no one can take without consent.

Femininity, Confidence, and Appearance

Femininity and confidence are intricately linked. A woman who carries her energy well doesn't need to speak to demand attention; the room tunes itself to her frequency. But this is not innate for all. Some of us spend years learning to silence the inner voice that apologizes, justifies, or diminishes our presence so that others feel comfortable. I learnt that my energy, my attention to my own alignment, my ability to read a room and respond without bending, was more powerful than any argument I could have made. Confidence becomes a companion to femininity when it is rooted in self-respect rather than performance. The two cannot be separated if you want your presence to be felt without being overwhelming, or ignored without being disrespected.

THE SELF-POSSESSED SHIELD

Let me tell you about the type of presence I admire; a woman who doesn't necessarily have to speak much in meetings, but when she does, her words land, and people literally would have no choice but to lean in. Her body language is deliberate and steady, as is her energy. I've gotten to realize that femininity is not a costume or an aesthetic choice, rather it is an internal standard. It's about the way a woman manages her energy, expectations, and her boundaries. And also having a contrast with others in the room which makes her remarkable.

When I began to consciously regulate my energy and treat my femininity as an internal frequency rather than an accessory, I noticed subtle but significant changes. Conversations that used to drain me no longer did. People began to treat me differently, and this wasn't because I had changed who I was, but because I had made my presence non-negotiable. I had allowed my energy to set the terms. There was a shift. People stopped assuming they could overstep or dismiss me. It was never about being harsh or inaccessible; it was about carrying a standard that did not require explanation.

Feminine energy, I realized, is also intimately tied to boundaries. It's impossible to maintain alignment without knowing where you end and others begin. I've learned that you cannot be fully receptive if your edges are undefined, nor can you maintain your shield if you are constantly defending yourself. And you cannot expect the world to adjust to your standards if you haven't adjusted to them yourself.

I have watched countless women operate in the world without understanding this, and I've seen how quickly exhaustion sets in. It's like trying to swim while holding onto sandbags. Your energy is diffused, and the room responds accordingly.

Appearance also plays a role in how feminine energy is perceived. Presentation is not superficial. It is an extension of the frequency you carry. When you look put together, you are signaling to yourself and to the world that your energy matters. I've experienced this countless times, from classmates who asked incredulously how I found the time to get ready in nursing school, to patients who took a liking to my appearance. Presentation is not about vanity but communicating standards. I've also had to navigate how femininity is often misread. Many

people, especially women, assumed that my attention to appearance and self-possesiveness meant I was fragile, or less capable, or even vain. These assumptions were wrong every single time. But they were instructive.
They taught me that feminine energy often challenges outdated assumptions of competence and professionalism.

People are conditioned to expect a certain kind of seriousness that has no room for grace, care, or attentiveness to self. That's why so many women learn to shrink or mask their energy, just because they believe it is safer to disappear than to be misunderstood. But then, disappearing is exhausting and depleting. It teaches the wrong lesson: that you must hide your energy to survive.

You do not need to hide. You simply need to carry it with awareness. You learn how to be receptive without being drained, how to assert your presence without aggression. You learn how to let the world respond to you, rather than demanding it through performance.

There is a subtle power in feminine energy that is often overlooked. It is consistent and difficult to measure. People sense it before they understand it. It is in how you hold your attention, how you regulate your voice, and how you choose to show up even when others might be dismissive. It isn't about being accommodating for its own sake. It is about being deliberate, conscious, and aligned. The room adjusts not because you demanded it, but because you carry yourself in a way that leaves no other option.

Ultimately, feminine energy is a practice of presence. It is a lifetime of learning how to inhabit your own frequency, how to honor your inner voice, and how to carry your standards as naturally as breathing. It is the understanding that being a woman does not equal weakness, and awareness is not vulnerability, nor is attention performance.

When this understanding takes root, it changes everything, and it won't only be about how the world responds to you, but how you respond to yourself.

CHAPTER 2
Feeling Good as a Non-Negotiable

Feeling good has never really been presented to most women as a right, but rather a framed reward, like something you get to earn after everyone else is satisfied and settled. Let me give an obvious example; You tend to feel good when the house is in order, when work is done, or when the kids are okay (if they are kids), or possibly when no one needs anything from you. And even then, you are expected to enjoy it briefly, without lingering too long in the comfort of it. Somewhere along the line, many of us learned to associate feeling good with guilt. As though ease was suspicious, and joy needed justification, and the rest had to be deserved. Alright fine, you could actually get taken care of, but never at the expense of someone else's comfort, and definitely not before everyone else's needs had been addressed.

This is the part of womanhood that is rarely spoken about honestly. The silent pressure to be emotionally available at all times, and the unspoken rule that your well-being must always

THE SELF-POSSESSED SHIELD

come second, that your job is to regulate the room, not yourself. I've come to learn that this conditioning is one of the fastest ways feminine energy gets depleted. Femininity does not thrive in a body that is constantly overriding itself. It doesn't survive long in a woman who is always adjusting, accommodating, postponing herself. And yet, this is the very posture many women are praised for. The one who endures, sacrifices, and is always there. We clap for her strength. We rarely ask what it's costing her.

For a long time, I believed that being a good woman meant being emotionally generous to everyone else first. I thought it was noble to be the last on my own list, that it was maturity and love. But what no one prepared me for was how quickly that posture turns into resentment. How easily it dulls your joy. How it slowly disconnects you from yourself until you are functional, dependable, and deeply tired. This is where the conversation about feeling good becomes uncomfortable. Because for many women, feeling good has been moralized. It has been turned into something that must be moderated, explained, or earned. If you are too intentional about your well-being, you are called selfish. If you prioritize yourself too openly, you are

THE SELF-POSSESSED SHIELD

accused of changing. If you choose ease, you are seen as unserious or lazy.

I come from a culture where endurance is often mistaken for virtue. Where suffering is romanticized, especially in women. Where you are taught that love requires sacrifice, and that sacrifice must hurt to be valid, where you need to suffer first before you can be sure that the product of the suffering was well deserved, especially if there was a smarter way to get the same result. For example, in most African homes, you're more "virtuous" if you can use your hands to wash a heap of clothes, especially if there is a washing machine option, and other more ridiculous tasks that can be made easier with machines. Your worth is weighed on how you can manage and be "understanding" and if you dare complain, you're reminded that other women endured worse. But comparison does not make exhaustion disappear. It only teaches you to ignore it.

What I began to notice, both in myself and in other women, was a pattern. The more disconnected a woman became from how she felt, the more effort she had to exert to maintain femininity. It became performative, smiles were forced, kindness felt obligatory, and femininity became something she acted out instead of something she inhabited. And this is where things start to fracture. Because feminine energy is not sustained by how much you give. It is sustained by how regulated you are internally. When you feel good, not temporarily distracted, not numbed, but genuinely well, your presence shifts. You move and speak differently, and you tend to listen without tension. You respond instead of reacting. People sense this before you say a word.

Your Emotions And You

Now this is the part that many people miss. Your emotional state is not private, it is broadcast. It might not necessarily be obvious or loud, but subtle. Your emotions could pass a message either through your tone, your posture, your patience, or your reactions. People feel it. They may not know what they're responding to, but they are responding nonetheless. This is why telling women to simply "be feminine" without addressing how they feel is incomplete advice. You cannot be convincingly feminine when your nervous system is in survival mode, or you're emotionally neglected, which sadly is the reality of most women. And yet, we are still encouraged to try.

There was a point in my life when I stopped seeing my emotions as something that happened to me and started seeing them as something that moved through me. That shift changed everything. I realized that how I felt was not just a private experience tucked away in my chest. It was something that traveled ahead of me, sat beside me, and lingered after I left a room. Whether I wanted it to or not, my emotional state was always speaking on my behalf. I used to think energy was an abstract concept, something people said when they didn't have the right words but over time, I began to notice patterns that were too consistent to ignore. Days when I felt grounded, and cared for, things simply flowed better, even inconveniences felt manageable. On days when I was tense, overwhelmed, or running on empty, everything felt louder. People seemed more demanding, the slightest of things did irritate me and I felt misunderstood more easily, but nothing about my environment had changed, what had come to play was how my emotions had been shaped that day. This is when it became clear to me that emotional states are not passive, they are active forces. They shape how we interpret the world and how the world responds to us. People often think communication begins when you open your mouth, but long before that happens, your body has already communicated. Your posture, your pace, your eyes, your breath. All of it is saying something.

Women are especially attuned to this, even if we don't always name it, our intuition is always more at peak way before normal logic. We sense tension when we walk into a room, we feel it when something is off, even when everyone is smiling, we notice shifts in tone that others brush past. This sensitivity is often framed as weakness or emotionality, even worse, they label us as superstitious and claim that we aren't factual. But I've come to learn that it's actually one of our greatest strengths, and it's a form of intelligence that doesn't rely on logic alone. The problem is that many women are taught to override this sensitivity. We are encouraged to push through discomfort, to ignore what our bodies are signaling, to silence our intuition in favor of being agreeable. And over time, that disconnection dulls our ability to regulate ourselves emotionally. We become reactive instead of responsive. We stay in situations that drain us because we've learned not to trust what we feel.

Feeling good then is not about chasing happiness or pretending everything is fine. It's about being regulated enough to hear yourself clearly, and tending to your inner state so that you're not constantly operating from depletion. When your nervous system is restful, your femininity settles into itself. It stops feeling like something you have to perform. I noticed this most clearly in my work. In healthcare, emotions are high. People are vulnerable. Fear, pain, and uncertainty sit heavy in the air. Early on, I learnt that no matter how skilled you are, if you walk into that space carrying anxiety or frustration, patients feel it. They may not articulate it, but they respond to it. They become tense, less trusting, and more guarded. And believe me, this can play a big role in the progress of their health at that moment; a well-relaxed patient will definitely respond to treatment, better and faster than an anxious one, because of the difference in energy used in attending to them. On days when I felt steady and emotionally cared for, the atmosphere shifted. Patients relaxed, conversations softened and there was less resistance, even when delivering difficult information. It wasn't because I said anything differently, but because my presence was different. This taught me something that stayed with me. Feeling good is not just for you, it is relational, and it affects the people around you in ways that are subtle but powerful. Your energy sets a tone. It permits others to either exhale or puts them on edge. And this is not about responsibility in a burdensome sense, it's about awareness.

When you feel good, genuinely good, you move through the world with a certain ease. You are less hurried, less defensive, and less reactive and you don't need to control situations as much because you trust yourself to handle them as they come. That trust is felt by others and it creates a sense of safety that has nothing to do with authority or dominance. This is where the misunderstanding around self-care often shows up. People reduce it to surface-level indulgence or dismiss it as vanity. But what they miss is that caring for yourself is a form of emotional hygiene. Just as you would not neglect your physical cleanliness and expect to feel well, you cannot neglect your emotional and energetic state and expect to move through life gracefully.

THE SELF-POSSESSED SHIELD

I began to see grooming, rest, and intentional environments differently. They were not extras, they were stabilizers. And whenever I took care of my appearance, it wasn't about being seen, it was mainly about feeling aligned. When my surroundings were calm and ordered, my mind followed. When I rested properly, my patience expanded and these things were not cosmetic, they were foundational.

There is a reason why women who feel good seem to attract better experiences without trying. It's not magic, it's coherence. Their internal state matches what they desire externally, and they are not asking the world to fill a void, rather they are meeting the world from a place of fullness. This is also why telling women to simply put others first without considering their emotional state is short-sighted. A depleted woman may still show up, but she does so at a cost. Over time, that cost accumulates. As a woman, feeling good is a responsibility, not in a punitive sense, but in a self-honoring one. It requires attention, honesty, and for you to stop dismissing your needs as secondary. And don't get me wrong, this doesn't mean you abandon care for others, it only means you stop abandoning yourself in the process.

I've come to learn that femininity flourishes when a woman is internally well, and not when she is constantly giving from an empty place, or running on obligation. It flourishes when she feels good; her aura becomes stable, her kindness is genuine and her presence is grounding. And this is where the shift begins. When feeling good stops being something you wait for and starts being something you cultivate, when you realize that tending to your emotional state is not selfish, but strategic, and when you understand that how you feel is not incidental, but influential. From there, everything else starts to rearrange itself naturally.

How Does Self-care Regulate?

This internal state is supported and maintained through the way you care for yourself physically and externally, and why grooming and presentation are not shallow acts, but deeply regulating ones. I've come to understand that when you take the time to tend to yourself, you are sending a very clear signal, to yourself first,

THE SELF-POSSESSED SHIELD

and to the world second that your well-being matters. It is a strategic, yet powerful declaration, that you are worth attention, care, and intention. This is why grooming isn't vanity, and why looking polished isn't about seeking approval. It is about anchoring yourself in your own value before anyone else can influence it. Think of it like energetic hygiene, just as you would wash your hands to protect your body from germs, grooming and tending to yourself protects your energy from drainage. A woman who takes care of her appearance, who sets aside space to rest, who moves through ordered surroundings, isn't just maintaining aesthetics, she is calibrating her frequency. When your nails are clean, your hair is tended to, your skin is nourished, your clothing fits and feels intentional, something shifts internally. You stand taller, your posture aligns, your breathing relaxes, and your nervous system signals that everything is good to go. It is a subtle, internal regulation that prepares you to move through the world without depletion and without constantly reacting to others.

I remember a particular pattern I noticed growing up Nigerian, which was always a beautiful sight to behold. Women around me were always investing in themselves, their hair, skin, beautifying their faces as they deemed fit, and clothing that fitted their body type. But it was not for anyone else. It was never about attracting men or winning approval. It was about how they felt in their own skin, the internal lift that came from looking intentional, clean, and put together. I saw this repeated everywhere, not for a date or a man's comment, but because they felt complete when they were cared for and presented. Because trust me, a proper Nigerian woman will look good, even if she's just going to a nearby shop to get groceries.

Your environment works the same way. Living spaces that are cluttered, chaotic, or draining can immediately unsettle your nervous system. And that part of self-care isn't just about what you do to yourself, but what surrounds you. A well-organized space, a clean room, soothing scents, or even just a corner where you can retreat, contribute to an internal state of restfulness. It's a feedback loop, that says your energy affects your space, and your space affects your energy. When you combine intentional self-care with a nurturing environment, your internal regulation becomes almost effortless. You aren't constantly draining yourself trying to maintain composure because your surroundings are supporting you. The ripple effect is undeniable. When you feel good internally, that energy radiates outward. Patients, clients, friends, even strangers sense it. You don't have to announce it, you just move differently, your presence shifts, and interactions flow more smoothly. Grooming, self-care, and environment are not indulgences, they are strategic acts of preservation. They are how you protect your feminine energy and keep it stable, so your femininity isn't performative but natural and sustained and you don't also get to fade under the weight of people's expectations.

In essence, self-care, grooming, and environment are not accessories to your femininity, they are the infrastructure. When you tend to them, you are not just "looking good," you are aligning your internal frequency with how you want to exist in the world. You are regulating yourself so your energy can flow freely, gracefully, and powerfully, creating an unshakable base for every other part of your life.

The Frequency You Carry Travels Ahead of You

THE SELF-POSSESSED SHIELD

One thing I've come to learn is that people feel you before they understand you. Before your words land. Before your credentials are explained. Your emotional state arrives first. When you are depleted, it shows. Not because you are physically weak, but because exhaustion has a scent, no matter how hard you try to mask it. It makes you sharper than you intend to be and more reactive than you recognize; you could snap over the slightest, making you "overreact". But when you feel good, truly good, resourced, rested, tended to, your presence becomes an invitation rather than a demand. This is why feeling good cannot be postponed indefinitely, and it is not a reward for survival, it is a requirement for sustainability. I have seen women light up rooms simply by being settled within themselves. And I have also seen others shrink, not because they lacked beauty or intelligence, but because they had learned to ignore their own needs for too long. Feminine energy only thrives where self-betrayal ends.

In our society, there is a complicated relationship with women investing in themselves. Beauty is celebrated, yet self-prioritization is often questioned. Why are you over performing? Who are you trying to impress? Meanwhile, the same women are expected to pour endlessly into families, workplaces, and communities without complaint. And when you get to look like what you're going through, the same society gets to criticize and ask you why you always look like what you're going through. It's funny how hypocritical the system is. Whatever you do to please the opinion of people and displease yourself, always has one end, you lose yourself, till you're unrecognizable to yourself.

Choose yourself, get in tune with your emotions and internal energy, do what makes you feel good about yourself, and the world will have no choice but to get in line.

Putting yourself first is strategic, not selfish!

This is the part many women struggle with. The idea that prioritizing your wellbeing somehow diminishes your goodness. That caring for yourself takes something away from others. I've learnt the opposite. When you feel good, you give better, not more, but better, and with less resentment and clearer boundaries. You even tend to give more presence, your patience stretches, your generosity becomes intentional, and your "No" becomes cleaner and more audible, without having to explain why. Feeling good sharpens your discernment. It helps you notice when something is off before it becomes unbearable. It gives you the clarity to step back instead of burning out. And it teaches you that your peace is not something to apologize for.

Putting yourself first is not an act of selfishness, it is an investment in how you engage with the world. I've come to realize that when women deny themselves, when we consistently put others' needs before our own, we aren't demonstrating love or maturity, we're just depleting our energy banks until there's nothing left to give. It's like trying to pour water from an empty cup. No matter how beautiful the gesture, it will always feel strained, forced, or incomplete. On the other hand, when you nurture yourself first, when you create space for your own alignment, everything you offer flows naturally. Your kindness is no longer performative. Your presence becomes stabilizing. Always remember that you can't save a drowning person if you're drowning yourself.

Do not get me wrong, it's not about indulgence either. You should take time in the spa. It's okay to treat yourself when you need it, but do not also ignore your responsibilities. Align your energy so that you move through life from fullness rather than depletion. When your internal state is stable, you're not constantly reacting to crises, micro-stresses, or other people's emotional baggage. You have a reservoir of clarity and patience that allows you to respond rather than react. You notice things others miss, and your decisions come from being centered.

I've observed this in women around me. Some are constantly "on" for everyone else; friends, colleagues, family, and yet appear exhausted, irritable, and reactive. Then some women invest in themselves regularly, through small acts of rest, grooming, or setting boundaries and the difference is visible. Not just in how they look, though that is part of it, but in how they move, how they speak, how they are treated. People instinctively trust them. They are taken seriously. They are listened to. Their energy precedes them, and the world responds accordingly. Feeling good first also teaches discernment. When you are aligned with your needs, you start recognizing environments, interactions, and relationships that drain you.

You notice the people who expect more than they give, the ones who dismiss your boundaries, and the spaces that leave you depleted. And instead of silently enduring or over-explaining, you begin to step back, make clearer choices, and protect your energy without guilt. It becomes less about proving yourself to anyone and more about honoring yourself consistently.

Ultimately, prioritizing yourself is strategic because it enhances everything you do. It makes your giving intentional, your presence impactful, and your boundaries firm but graceful. It allows you to navigate the world without losing your joy. And once you understand this, self-care stops being optional or indulgent; it becomes essential. Not only for your well-being, but for how effectively you move through life, influence people, and maintain your feminine energy. When you feel good, your femininity does not have to work so hard. It simply exists. And that existence alone changes how the world responds to you.

CHAPTER 3
Advocacy Wrapped in Grace

When I was much younger, whenever I heard someone talk about speaking up, what I had in mind was that it had a specific shape, a sharp edge, maybe a raised voice, or a hardness that women were warned against early on. Growing up, one of the subtle messages that was so pushed onto our faces was that the woman who endured was praised, while the one who spoke plainly was corrected. Silence was called grace, and compliance was mistaken for maturity. And like most girls, I learnt how to make myself smaller without being asked directly. What I didn't realize then was how much silence costs over time. It doesn't happen overnight but slowly it builds, settles in the body, in the heart, and mind until you start finding yourself rehearsing conversations before they are had, you find yourself learning how to tolerate things that you shouldn't because it feels easier than being misunderstood.

Honestly, one thing women should be aware of, is the fact that peace that's built on self-erasure isn't peace at all but postponement. There is a deep myth around femininity that says being feminine must come with passivity. That to be graceful, you must be agreeable, and that firmness automatically makes you abrasive, and I believed this for a long time, until life proved otherwise. I watched how my needs didn't disappear just because I didn't voice them, they only became heavier and then, the moments I finally spoke, the discomfort in the room wasn't caused by my tone, but by the boundary itself. We need to come to the understanding that respect does not require volume, but it does require presence, and you can say no without apology. The confusion often comes from people who benefit from your silence, and when you stop performing agreeableness, it unsettles them and that discomfort is often misnamed as you being difficult.

Culturally, women are taught to smooth things over, to manage and carry the emotional burdens that are not theirs, to absorb inconvenience and call it patience. In many spaces, especially familiar ones, a woman advocating for herself is treated as an anomaly. Questions are asked, and motives are doubted, you are suddenly "overly emotional." Yet, the same environment has no issue placing endless demands on your time, your energy, your body, your emotional labor. In Nigerian culture especially, women are expected to accommodate endlessly, to smile through discomfort, to smooth over tension, and to bend without breaking. The moment you assert yourself or refuse to tolerate disrespect, the labels start appearing, "problematic," "too much," "unreasonable," or worse, the dreaded "Karen" equivalent. I've seen it happen repeatedly, not just to me, but to women around me. And it's always fascinating because the same society that critiques this boldness will simultaneously admire it in secret, wishing they could claim a fraction of that audacity for themselves. Being called difficult is not a verdict on your character, it is a signal that you are shifting the energy, that you are disrupting expectations. It's a recognition, subtle though it may be, that you are no longer playing small to make others comfortable.

People are used to women who adjust, who defer, who politely absorb and tolerate. When you refuse to shrink, it can make others uncomfortable, and discomfort often translates into labels. But you should know that discomfort is not inherently negative, it's the indicator that you are stepping into a space that has long been off-limits to you, your own autonomy, your self-respect, and your voice. Don't let anyone tell you otherwise. However, the key is how you respond. You don't have to harden, yell, or become combative. Advocacy wrapped in grace is about maintaining composure while staying firm. It's about being aware that someone's opinion of you does not diminish your value.

The lesson to be learnt here might be subtle but vital, being labeled difficult is often a precursor to being respected. It's also worth noting that this label carries a certain freedom. Once you accept that advocating for yourself may provoke criticism, you stop shrinking in advance. You move through life more intentionally, choosing your battles, curating your environment, and honoring your standards without waiting for approval. The audacity to be unapologetic becomes an internal shield. It is imperative to master this.

So, always have in mind that being labeled difficult is not a failure but evidence that you are doing exactly what you are meant to do, which is protecting your boundaries, asserting your needs, and living fully in alignment with yourself. It is a badge of authenticity, and the sooner you stop shrinking from it, the sooner you experience the power of advocacy wrapped in grace. I've come to accept that being perceived as the problem is sometimes the price of no longer being one. Choosing self-respect over approval, doesn't necessarily need to be loud, It can be deliberate, and steady. It looks like holding eye contact, not over-explaining, and walking away when a conversation starts requiring you to betray yourself.

Grace, I've learned, is not about shrinking. It is about being so anchored in yourself that you don't need to harden to be firm and that kind of advocacy does not take away from femininity. It returns you to it.

How to Exude Grace While Advocating for Yourself

Grace has long been mistaken for silence, especially when it comes to women. We are taught that composure means compliance, that maturity looks like endurance, and that peace is preserved by swallowing our discomfort. We are praised for being accommodating, for smiling through what should be questioned, and for staying silent even when something feels wrong. Over time, silence becomes framed not just as a choice, but as a moral virtue. But grace is not the absence of a voice. And silence, when practiced without intention, can turn into self-betrayal.

When you consistently withhold your truth to avoid conflict or disapproval, you begin to erode your own needs, desires, and standards. What starts as peacekeeping slowly becomes a habit of self-erasure. You adjust, explain less, ask for less, expect less, until you are no longer sure where your boundaries end and other people's comfort begins.

The irony is that this kind of silence is celebrated only as long as it serves others. Society applauds endurance until it becomes inconvenient. The moment you assert a boundary, say no, or visibly choose yourself, the narrative shifts. Suddenly, you are labeled difficult, ungrateful, dramatic, or problematic. Not because you are wrong, but because you have disrupted an unspoken agreement that benefited everyone except you.

Grace, on the other hand, does not mean shrinking. It means standing firmly without becoming hardened. It means speaking with intention rather than reacting from anger or fear. When you enforce a boundary and feel tension rise, that discomfort is not a sign of wrongdoing. It is a signal that you are exercising agency. You are rewriting invisible rules that once demanded your silence.

There are two kinds of silence. One is chosen from fear or guilt, designed to keep you palatable and unchallenging. This silence drains you. The other is chosen from self-respect and clarity. This silence is powerful. It is deliberate. It allows you to pause, assess, and respond rather than explain yourself endlessly.

Exuding grace while advocating means knowing when to speak and when to withhold, not to protect others from discomfort, but to protect your integrity. It is the ability to say what needs to be said without cruelty, to hold your ground without apology, and to remain composed even when others feel unsettled by your growth.

True grace lives in this balance. It is not found in obedience or self-sacrifice, but in alignment.

When your words, boundaries, and actions reflect your self-worth, you stop confusing peace with silence and start understanding that dignity sometimes makes noise. And when it does, let it.

Differentiating Aggression from Firmness & Passiveness from Tenderness

There's a difference between asserting yourself from a grounded, regulated place and reacting from tension or defensiveness. Firmness comes from clarity and confidence. It doesn't require shouting, demanding, or making someone else feel small. A firm woman knows what she stands for, communicates it without apology, and holds her space without needing to dominate or intimidate. Aggression, on the other hand, is often fueled by frustration, fear, or impatience. It can come across as sharp, reactive, or overbearing, and it tends to push people away rather than command respect. The key distinction is that firm energy carries authority, while aggression carries reactive intensity.

Similarly, being tender versus passive is about intention and presence. Tenderness is a strength, not an absence of strength. It allows you to remain receptive, attuned, very feminine, and emotionally intelligent while still maintaining boundaries. Feminine women can listen, empathize, and respond thoughtfully without diminishing themselves. Passiveness, however, is a retreat from responsibility or self-advocacy, it is ignoring your needs or desires to avoid conflict or discomfort. A passive person may appear agreeable, but their energy is often uncertain, ungrounded, and easily swayed. Tenderness without passivity is deliberate, passivity masquerades as compliance but erodes your energy over time.

Tone is often misread through bias. A woman speaking clearly and assertively may be labeled "harsh" or "difficult," whereas a man in the same situation is seen as confident or authoritative. This misperception reinforces why regulation matters more than volume. Your power isn't in how loudly you speak or how visibly forceful you appear, it's in how composed, intentional, and aligned your energy is when you engage. A regulated woman communicates her boundaries, expresses her needs, and navigates conflict without reacting impulsively.

That kind of energy is persuasive, magnetic, and lasting, because it comes from an internal steadiness rather than external pressure or performance. Understanding these distinctions helps women realize that advocacy and grace are not opposites. You can remain tender, composed, and feminine while being unyielding about your standards. Likewise, firmness doesn't require aggression or hostility, it only demands clarity, consistency, and emotional regulation. Recognizing this allows you to operate in the world with influence without sacrificing your essence or permitting others to misread your strength.

Advocacy without apology is about the energy you carry when you speak up for yourself. It begins internally, with the posture you hold in your own mind and body. When you are clear about what you want, what you need, and what you will accept, there's no urge to over-explain or justify yourself. Over-explaining often comes from insecurity or the fear of being judged, but when your internal standard is strong, you trust that your boundaries and requests are valid without needing external validation. Grace in advocacy isn't about performance or being "nice." It is a grounded certainty that communicates your position firmly but without aggression. Your voice, your body language, and your energy align with your intent. You don't have to raise your tone to be heard, and you don't have to lighten your message to avoid backlash.

Clarity creates authority. When you know exactly what you want and why it matters to you, your confidence shows naturally, and others respond to that energy more readily than to words alone. This grounded certainty also allows you to navigate moments of conflict strategically. There's a rhythm to speaking your truth, you know when to engage and when to step back, when persistence is productive and when walking away is the wiser choice. You advocate not from reaction but from intention, which is why your presence feels controlled, strong, and unshakable even in tense situations. People may label you as "difficult" or "uncompromising," but that's a reflection of their expectations, not your character.

I've learned that trusting yourself internally reduces the need to defend externally. Once your posture is anchored in self-respect, saying "no," correcting mistakes, or requesting better treatment becomes simple, almost effortless. You don't need to justify or apologize because your energy communicates your worth before your words ever land. Advocacy without apology is the practice of embodying your standards fully, so that firmness and femininity coexist naturally. It's not about being unyielding for the sake of conflict; it's about honoring yourself while still moving through the world with poise, influence, and undeniable presence.

Health, Wellness & Feminine Self-Advocacy

Health and wellness are more than physical states, they are expressions of self-love, and they form one of the clearest ways a woman can advocate for herself. When you prioritize what you eat, how you move, and the rhythms of your daily life, you are sending a signal that says that your needs, energy, and standards matter, first to yourself, and then to the world.

In many ways, these choices become boundary markers. When you decide to rest, to nourish your body intentionally, or to create space for movement that feels good, you are drawing a line between what is for you and what is for everyone else. You are telling the universe that

THE SELF-POSSESSED SHIELD

you are a woman whose energy is valuable, whose time is not infinite, and whose presence deserves to be respected.

In my own life, this became evident during travel or when navigating situations outside of familiar routines. I remember while visiting one of the countries in South America and I quickly realized that the local cuisine was heavily centered around carbs, with very few vegetable-rich options. My lifestyle, however, is keto-based, high in protein, and full of clean vegetables. I could have shrugged and eaten what was convenient, but I knew that compromising on my standards would leave me feeling off, both physically and energetically. Instead, I went to a local supermarket, selected the ingredients that aligned with my diet, and asked the hotel staff to prepare my meals accordingly. Some of them looked at me with the familiar expression many confident women, especially Nigerian women, know well, the silent "Who does she think she is?" judgment. I didn't shrink, I simply maintained my poise, knowing that my commitment was to myself first. My health, my energy, and my boundaries were non-negotiable. Also, the hotel didn't have a gym, but that didn't stop me either. I made sure to hit my 12,000 to 15,000 steps every single day. No excuses or compromise. My choices were intentional, not to prove a point to anyone or to seek approval. They were about protecting my energy, maintaining my standards, and honoring how I wanted to feel.

It wasn't about impressing anyone, and I didn't apologize for it. It was about my body, my energy, and my commitment to myself. In that moment, every choice I made about what I ate, how I moved, and how I prioritized rest, was advocacy in action. It was feminine because it was done with intention, grace, and respect for my own needs.

The same applies to daily routines. Choosing to sleep when your body needs it, moving in ways that feel expansive, and tending to rituals that stabilize your mind and mood are not indulgent or selfish. They are statements of self-regard. When you invest in wellness, you are actively managing your internal state. A woman who is nourished, rested, and moving intentionally is less reactive, less drained, and more capable of enforcing her boundaries without guilt or aggression. Her advocacy is embedded in her lifestyle, it doesn't require confrontation to assert itself. Wellness also becomes a protective framework.

If your energy is scattered, your boundaries are fuzzy, and your emotional availability is stretched thin, it is easy for others' expectations and demands to overwhelm you. But when you prioritize your health and well-being, your body and mind serve as anchors. You move through life with greater clarity, resilience, and presence. You don't just respond, but you do that with intention. Your self-care routines, your dietary choices, your sleep habits, and even the way you move through space all become subtle but powerful forms of advocacy. They remind you, and remind others, that your time and energy are yours to steward.

In essence, prioritizing wellness is not about control over others or perfection in your lifestyle. It's about being loyal to yourself, creating the conditions where your feminine energy can thrive, and communicating without words that your life is guided by your standards, your needs, and your values. The act of caring for your body, mind, and environment is advocacy in its most graceful form: it protects your energy, reinforces your boundaries, and keeps your presence vibrant, coherent, and unmistakably yours.

This is the principle of advocacy wrapped in grace. You don't need to argue, raise your voice, or justify your choices to anyone. Your internal alignment, your consistency, and your willingness to prioritize yourself send a clear message about your standards. Others might label you as "difficult" or "demanding," but that says nothing about you and everything about how they perceive boundaries they are not accustomed to respecting. By taking care of yourself in visible, intentional ways, through your choices, your habits, and your self-prioritization, you advocate for yourself gracefully. You communicate that your well-being matters, that your standards are non-negotiable, and that your presence is a space of stability and clarity, not chaos or compromise.

Remember:

Advocating for yourself can feel uncomfortable at first, especially in spaces where women are expected to be agreeable. You need to know that being firm about what you need does not make

THE SELF-POSSESSED SHIELD

you unkind or unfeminine, rather, it simply means you understand your value and will not let others diminish it. You can speak with tenderness and still enforce your boundaries, you can correct, redirect, or decline without raising your voice or losing your power. The discomfort others feel is often a reflection of their own expectations, not a measure of your behavior. Choosing yourself may make you appear difficult and that is okay. That label does not define your worth, it often signals that you are advocating correctly.

The principle is simple; you cannot expect others to honor your boundaries if you do not honor them yourself first. Curating your life to align with your values and needs is not arrogance, it is intentional living. Speaking up, correcting the service you receive, or adjusting circumstances to suit your wellness does not make you ungrateful or difficult. It makes you consistent. It teaches the world how to treat you, and it reinforces your own internal alignment. Knowing when to speak and when to walk away is really about discernment. It's the skill of recognizing which battles are worth your energy and which are not.

Walking away is about choosing to protect your peace, your energy, and your integrity, and not about weakness or avoidance. It is a decision rooted in emotional maturity, where you understand that asserting yourself does not always mean confronting every slight, challenge, or inconvenience. Speaking up should happen when your boundaries are crossed, when your values are compromised, or when clarity is required. Walking away becomes the feminine response when the situation no longer aligns with your standards, or when engagement would drain rather than build. It is not passive; it is an active choice that preserves your presence and maintains your frequency. The act of walking away signals that your energy cannot be borrowed or depleted for situations that disrespect or undervalue you.

Discernment here is subtle. It's the ability to feel whether your contribution will create progress or unnecessary conflict. It's also about understanding the context and potential impact of your voice. Sometimes, silence paired with strategic withdrawal communicates more strength than words ever could. When you choose to speak or step back, both actions carry power. Both require self-awareness, self-respect, and the courage to act in alignment with your well-being. Ultimately, knowing when to engage and when to retreat reframes how you inhabit your femininity. It is not about shrinking or giving up. It is about balancing assertiveness with grace and understanding that your presence and energy are finite resources. You give where it matters most and conserve where it does not. This discernment is a cornerstone of advocacy wrapped in grace, teaching that influence is not measured by volume, but by intentionality and the alignment of your actions with your values.

Tenderness does not require surrender, grace does not demand silence, and advocacy does not have to be loud or aggressive. The power lies in clarity, consistency, and the confidence that comes from knowing exactly what you need and choosing to protect it. When you act with that combination of intention and care, you realize that advocating for yourself is not a rebellion; it is an extension of femininity lived fully and unapologetically.

CHAPTER 4
Refusing to Shrink

I can't overemphasize it enough, that until women finally get to see it for what it is; as women, the world, the society is so patriarchal, that they've normalized convincing women to make themselves smaller, constantly demanding that we dim ourselves to make others comfortable; and the funny part? Most women have not only accepted this madness, but they ensure it's enforced on the younger generation of women, shoved down our throats, and tell us that, that's how the system has always been and there's nothing we can do about it.

I mean, even how we dress is also a negotiation, and how we dress isn't judged on the fact that we do it for ourselves, but it's somehow implied that our reasons can be of no other than trying to please the other gender, and for so long that's the ideology that has been imposed in our society, and it's crazy. I mean how more obvious can they get about wanting the world to always revolve around them? And this conditioning doesn't always arrive as a loud command, it comes with a well-programmed manipulation and gaslighting scheme, that has been imposed in the system a long time ago, to ensure that the mental hold they have on us stands. It often comes as tiny, repeated instructions, it could be a comment from an aunt about dressing modestly, a teacher telling you not to "show off," a colleague or family member questioning why you spoke up or made an effort to look your best. Over time, these small nudges become internalized as rules. We learn to shrink in multiple dimensions, physically, verbally, aesthetically, and emotionally, so that we are tolerable, non-threatening, and safe in the eyes of those around us.

The problem is that shrinking isn't just a habit, it's an erasure of self, and overtime, when the gaslighting scheme has been perfected and imbibed in our heads, we bend to the patriarchal society rules and then, we begin to apologize for the very things that make us visible; our presence, our competence, our polish, our beauty. And the irony is that the more we shrink, the more invisible we feel, even as others continue to benefit from our labor, our intellect, our care. We become experts at minimizing ourselves, trading authentic

THE SELF-POSSESSED SHIELD

expressions for social comfort. I've come to understand that confidence doesn't exist in that space of self-diminishment. It begins the moment we refuse to shrink, when we reclaim the right to take up space in the world without hesitation or apology.

I want you to always have in mind that confidence is not loudness for the sake of attention, you don't need to shout to be heard or noticed, that's actually a tacky behaviour, neither is confidence rebellion dressed up as performance, you don't need to be extra dramatic just to prove you're confident, over playing that role can make one look like a clown and it's embarrassing. Rather, confidence doesn't need announcement, it is steady and unwavering. It is deciding that your presence, your voice, your choices, your appearance, and your efforts all matter, simply because you exist and have value. Walking into a room polished, poised, and intentional is not a provocation, it is a declaration of standard. And yes, it will draw attention (the necessary type of attention), sometimes admiration, and most sometimes resentment, because society detests when they can't control you anymore, but that attention says far more about others than it does about you.

Refusing to shrink is not defiance for the sake of defiance, it is alignment with your own worth, it is choosing yourself when the culture has conditioned you to prioritize everyone else first. It is honoring your presence in a world that expects women to be secondary and diminutive.

The first step in refusing to shrink is awareness. It is noticing the ways you have unconsciously minimized yourself to make others comfortable. The next is intention; deciding to take up the space that is rightfully yours without apology. And from there, everything else flows; your decisions, your confidence, your boundaries, your energy. Shrinking may have been conditioned, but standing tall is a choice, one that women are capable of making at any moment, and one that begins to reshape not just how others see us, but how we see ourselves.

Confidence begins the moment you refuse to shrink. Not letting anyone manipulate you into downplaying your achievements, just cause you want to make someone who's insecure feel good about themselves. If that's you, and you've been bending to their biddings, light has finally come your way, and I urge you, sis, take your space, make them insecure, make them uncomfortable, wear your accomplishments like a badge, dress in the best way that makes you feel comfortable and what you believe is your style, do not let the patriarchy win. Stop shrinking for them to shine. And from now on, start walking into any room you step into, fully prepared, well-presented, polished, and intentional, that's an act of claiming space, and it's not provocation, but a standard. And always have it at the back of your mind, that when you do this, reactions are inevitable, and that's expected. Admiration comes, but so does resentment. The questions follow. "Why are you so dressed up?" "Who are you trying to impress?" "Don't you think that's too much?" These questions are never really about you. They are about the insecurities, limitations, and expectations of the person asking. I have learned to recognize this quickly and I have stopped justifying my standards. I show up for myself first. Their discomfort is not my responsibility.

There is a particular hostility reserved for women who combine competence with beauty. A polished, capable woman disrupts expectations. Society is comfortable with one or the other, but not both. To be competent and look put together is often to invite subtle judgment or skepticism. Early in my career, I experienced this repeatedly. Colleagues questioned my knowledge or expertise as a nurse, not because it was lacking, but because they could not reconcile it with the way I looked. My appearance was feminine, intentional, and polished. My capability was evident. The discomfort it caused others revealed their bias, not my inadequacy. I realized that refusing to shrink is not arrogance; it is confidence rooted in self-respect.

Confidence does not exist to make others comfortable. I have people in my life I no longer deal with because their behavior eroded my peace. Gaslighting, dismissiveness, or invalidating my emotions is not acceptable, regardless of who delivers it. Respect is felt in the small things, in acknowledgment, in listening, in honoring boundaries. My feelings are real, they exist, and they matter. Silence and avoidance do not resolve conflict. Swept-under emotions accumulate, harden, and corrode relationships. Maintaining your confidence means maintaining this standard in every interaction, including those with family. Blood ties do not grant permission to silence you, diminish you, or demand that you betray yourself. I have been asked, repeatedly, how I manage to look intentional and polished consistently. The answer is simple. It is a standard I hold for myself. Showing up well-prepared, presentable, and aesthetically intentional is a reflection of how I value myself. Others may misinterpret it, assume it requires extraordinary effort, or question my intentions, but it is not for them. My appearance is part of my internal regulation. It aligns my energy, supports my confidence, and reinforces the truth that I will not shrink to fit anyone else's comfort.

Being confident is not about approval, it is about refusing to apologize for your existence, your presence, or your choices. It is about honoring yourself fully, even when that disrupts expectations. Standing in your truth, maintaining your standards, and claiming your space are not acts of defiance. They are acts of alignment. They are how confidence, dignity, and femininity coexist without compromise.

The Silent Conditioning of Shrinking

There are many subtle ways society teaches women to shrink, and most of them are disguised as advice. Speak, but not too much. Be confident, but not intimidating. Dress well, but do not look like you are trying too hard. Be intelligent, but do not correct anyone publicly. Take up space, but not enough to make others uncomfortable. None of these rules is written down, yet women learn them early. They are reinforced at home, in school, in the workplace, and even among other women. Shrinking becomes a survival skill, not because women lack confidence, but because confidence is often punished when it is visible.

In professional spaces, this shrinking shows up in how women are expected to present themselves. A woman who is polished is questioned. An assertive woman is labeled difficult. A woman who is both prepared and well put together is often met with suspicion rather than respect. There is an unspoken expectation that seriousness must look a certain way, usually stripped of femininity or beauty. When a woman does not conform to that image, her competence is doubted. She is asked more questions. She is watched more closely. She is expected to prove herself repeatedly in ways others are not.

This does not happen because she is incapable. It happens because she has violated a narrow script. Society is comfortable with women being capable as long as they remain visually and energetically unthreatening. It is comfortable with beauty as long as it is detached from authority. When those two meet in one body, people scramble to place her. They look for flaws. They question her seriousness. They search for reasons to diminish what they cannot easily categorize.

Shrinking is also emotional. Women are taught to censor their reactions even when something is wrong. To smile through discomfort. To explain their boundaries gently so no one feels accused. To apologize before speaking, after speaking, and sometimes for simply existing in the room. Over time, this teaches women to mistrust their own responses. If something feels off, they are encouraged to rationalize it away. If something hurts, they are told they are being too sensitive. The message is consistent. Your comfort matters less than the atmosphere you maintain for others.

In Nigerian culture, shrinking is framed as respect. Do not challenge elders. Do not speak back. Do not disrupt peace. What is rarely acknowledged is that this peace often comes at the cost of one person swallowing themselves repeatedly. Silence is praised as maturity. Endurance is mistaken for strength. Boundaries are treated as rebellion. Over time, many women internalize the belief that love requires self-erasure.

But confidence begins where shrinking ends. It begins the moment a woman decides that her presence does not need to be apologized for. That her voice does not need to be diluted to be acceptable. That her appearance does not need to be toned down to be taken seriously. Refusing to shrink is not about dominance or defiance. It is about coherence. It is about allowing who you are internally to match how you show up externally.

When you stop shrinking, something settles. You no longer spend energy managing how you are perceived. You stop negotiating your standards. You allow yourself to be seen clearly, even if that visibility unsettles others. And it will. Not everyone benefits from a woman who is fully present, fully expressed, and fully anchored in herself. But that discomfort is not a signal to retreat. It is often a sign that something outdated is being challenged.

Refusing to shrink is an act of self-respect repeated daily. It is choosing not to dim your light to fit into rooms that were never built with your fullness in mind. It is understanding that your competence, your beauty, your voice, and your boundaries are not separate traits you must ration out carefully. They are parts of a whole. And you are allowed to exist as such.

When a woman stops shrinking, she does not become harsh. She becomes clear. She does not become selfish. She becomes honest. And in that honesty, confidence is no longer something she performs. It becomes something she inhabits.

Confidence is often framed as something that must be humble or unassuming, so as not to threaten anyone. True confidence does not negotiate, it does not shrink or apologize to make others comfortable. It is rooted in a clear understanding of your worth and an unwavering commitment to honoring yourself, regardless of external reactions. The challenge comes in applying this principle in real life, especially when family, friends, or colleagues attempt to invalidate your boundaries or minimize your achievements. There are moments when someone questions your choices, dismisses your accomplishments, or expects you to compromise your standards for their comfort. The instinct can be to justify yourself, to over-explain, or to dampen your stance. You have to understand that maintaining confidence means resisting that impulse, and standing firm does not make you unkind or harsh, rather it makes you self-respecting. Confidence also intersects deeply with femininity. A woman who knows her worth does not need to dim her light for anyone, even those closest to her. Honoring your boundaries, whether it means declining obligations that drain you, removing toxic influences, or refusing to tolerate gaslighting, is an act of self-preservation and feminine power. This can include family members whose patterns are harmful or dismissive. Removing someone from your life, even a relative, is not betrayal. It is a recognition that your peace, your energy, and your integrity are not negotiable.

I wish more people could realize that most of the time, family can be very entitled, and not only in and about the resources they expect you to provide, but also most of the time, they also want to play a big role in your decisions, and life in a whole. Like I said, and I'll always say, once you realise a choking entitlement from them in any aspect, please draw back and limit their access to you, because letting them ride you the way they please, it becomes toxic and draining, and you'll end up losing yourself, before you even realise it. In practical terms, this looks like setting limits without apology, like asserting your needs and refusing to allow others' discomfort to dictate your choices. It looks like being fully present in your life without shrinking to fit someone else's expectations. You do not need to tone down your success, your voice, or your presence to make anyone feel safe or comfortable. Confidence is not performative; it is firm, and consistent. It allows you to navigate your relationships with clarity and grace while keeping your internal energy intact.

Ultimately, the essence of this principle is that confidence is inseparable from self-respect. Honoring yourself, protecting your space, and refusing to compromise your values is not arrogance, but it is necessary. True confidence allows you to engage with the world fully, to pursue your ambitions without apology, and to maintain your feminine energy without dilution. It is a refusal to be diminished, a refusal to apologize for existing fully, and a commitment to living on your own terms.

Why Explain Yourself?

The idea of refusing to explain yourself centers on the freedom that comes from fully owning your choices, standards, and presence without needing external validation. It is the recognition that your life, your appearance, your effort, and your boundaries do not require justification to anyone else. This is especially relevant for women who are conditioned to constantly clarify their actions to avoid criticism or discomforting others. For example, imagine being questioned about why you spent time ensuring your outfit, makeup, or overall presentation is polished. Instead of responding defensively, you choose silence. That silence itself communicates the message that you value yourself, your standards are non-negotiable, and you are aligned with your own expectations, not theirs. Over time, consistently holding this posture communicates strength more effectively than words ever could. People learn that your standards are not up for debate, and your presence commands respect because it is grounded in self-alignment rather than performance for approval. Another instance is the effort you put into your work, whether it's professional, personal, or creative. In environments where overachievement is often questioned or labeled as "showing off" or "too much," explaining yourself diminishes your energy and subtly reinforces the idea that your excellence needs justification. By refusing to explain, you protect your energy and assert your boundaries firmly. This does not mean being dismissive or rude, it means being secure enough in your standards to let your work speak for itself while maintaining composure and dignity.

THE SELF-POSSESSED SHIELD

The freedom of not explaining yourself also extends to personal choices, like social interactions, dietary preferences, or lifestyle standards. When you no longer feel the need to rationalize why you exercise certain boundaries or pursue specific routines, you stop negotiating your self-worth in every interaction. Your consistent alignment sends a clear signal to others about what you accept and what you do not. It naturally filters out people who would drain you or challenge your autonomy, leaving space for relationships and environments that respect and support your values. It is important to note that refusing to explain yourself is not an act of defiance for its own sake. It is not about being difficult or uncooperative. It is about cultivating clarity within yourself so that your energy is preserved and your presence is powerful. By consistently refusing to justify your standards, you reinforce your internal authority. People will notice, sometimes with admiration, sometimes with resistance, but the difference is that your energy is now yours to steward. It no longer bends to meet the expectations of others. Ultimately, this practice strengthens femininity, confidence, and personal sovereignty. When you stop explaining yourself, you stop shrinking, apologizing, and diffusing your energy to make others comfortable. You move through the world fully aligned, and that alignment, more than anything else, communicates power, grace, and self-respect without uttering a single word.

This approach, applied consistently, ensures that your boundaries are respected, your standards are honored, and your presence is naturally commanding, making it a foundational skill for personal and professional growth.

Consistency and personal standards

Maintaining personal standards consistently is one of the most powerful ways to embody confidence and femininity. It is not about impressing anyone or performing for approval, but about holding yourself to a level of care, intention, and presence that signals your value first to yourself, and naturally to the world. This includes the small but meaningful acts, like taking time to dress thoughtfully, preparing thoroughly for tasks, showing up fully present, and attending to your appearance and environment.

Over time, these daily choices build an internal framework that tells your mind, body, and energy that you are worthy of investment. The key here is consistency. One polished day followed by a week of neglect does not cultivate the same energy as showing up with intention every day. Consistency trains not only your own internal frequency but also how others respond to you. When you maintain your standards, people start to recognize that you operate from a place of self-respect, and that respect is non-negotiable. It is in these moments that assumptions and judgments about you often arise. Someone may comment on your polished appearance and question your competence, as though beauty and capability cannot coexist. Their skepticism is never about you, but it is a reflection of their own biases and limitations. Their assumptions do not diminish your expertise, your skills, or your authority.

This is where the link between standards, confidence, and femininity becomes clear. Holding to your standards is an act of self-honoring. It signals to yourself that you are a person worthy of care and attention, and that you will not dilute your presence to make others comfortable. In doing so, you cultivate an energy that is simultaneously grounded, inviting, and powerful. Feminine energy thrives in women who have mastered this internal consistency because it allows warmth and poise to exist without compromise. When you know what you expect of yourself and follow through, you no longer have to perform to be seen as competent or respected. You simply are.

The daily discipline of maintaining standards may feel small, even mundane, but its cumulative effect is transformational. Dressing intentionally, preparing thoroughly, and showing up with awareness of your presence are acts that recalibrate your energy before the world ever interacts with it. Others may respond with admiration, curiosity, or even discomfort, but that is the natural outcome of standing firmly in your truth. Confidence is not about avoiding scrutiny or disapproval, it's just refusing to shrink in response to it. Every intentional act reinforces the message that your standards are yours alone, that they are self-respecting, and that you do not negotiate them for anyone. Ultimately, setting and maintaining personal standards is not a superficial exercise. It is a strategic and deeply feminine practice. It teaches your mind and

THE SELF-POSSESSED SHIELD

body what it means to value yourself, communicates to others what you accept and will not accept, and creates a foundation for every other area of your life. Your energy becomes coherent, your presence undeniable, and your boundaries unassailable. By consistently aligning with your standards, you ensure that your confidence is visible without effort, your femininity is expressed without compromise, and your life flows according to the priorities and values you have chosen, not the expectations of others.

When your life aligns with how it is meant to be, you will finally realize that the discomfort of someone else, just because you are a high flyer, is not your responsibility. When someone reacts negatively to your presence, your competence, or your elegance, it says more about them than it does about you. This understanding is liberating. You no longer have to explain why you take care of yourself, why you set boundaries, or why you insist on excellence in how you present and carry yourself. Freedom comes in realizing that your peace, your standards, and your energy are not negotiable. They are your inheritance, and maintaining them is a practice of honoring who you are. Your presence, polish, and competence are inseparable elements of your feminine energy. When you are aligned internally, your confidence becomes visible without effort, and you do not need to assert yourself aggressively or seek validation to be noticed. Your consistency and your standards command attention because they signal a woman who knows her worth and will not compromise it for approval.

Refusing to shrink also means choosing environments and relationships that support, rather than drain, you. It means selectively giving your energy to people who honor your boundaries and reflect your values. It is a form of advocacy for yourself wrapped in grace, the ability to protect your space without aggression and assert your presence without apology. This discipline does not diminish your femininity, it amplifies it. Feminine energy thrives when it is steady, intentional, and unshakable.

All being said, refusing to shrink is a radical act of self-respect. It is the conscious choice to live authentically, and to align your life with your standards, refusing to compromise your well-being for the comfort of others. The power in this is subtle but undeniable, it creates a life where your energy is coherent and your femininity exists as a force that is formidable. And also, when you align to what you're meant to be, you attract like minds and it makes the journey easier, because as humans, especially as women, we are emotional beings, and most of the time, opinions and scrutiny gets to us; so it's best if you have your community of like minds to be your anchor when you're just being human again.

CHAPTER 5
The Concept of Attraction

If you believe you deserve better, then the world will give it to you. However, the reality of things is that there is a specific kind of exhaustion that comes from trying to attract the life you want while being told that your worth is a moving target. We are often taught that attraction is an outward pull, a performance of beauty, a curation of personality, or a strategic display of "good woman" traits. But the truth is more than that. Attraction isn't something you do; it is a frequency you settle into. It is the steady, internal signal that tells the world exactly what you are willing to host in your space.

The world does not respond to what you need or even what you deserve in a moral sense. The world is responsive to what you expect. If you move through your days waiting for someone else to set the temperature of the room, you will always be at the mercy of their climate. But when you stabilize your own frequency, the room has no choice but to adjust to you.

THE SELF-POSSESSED SHIELD

We often confuse hope with expectation, but in reality, they are worlds apart. Hope is passive. It is the "good girl" posture we were taught, the one that waits in line, keeps its head down, and prays that someone in authority notices our patience and rewards us with respect. Hope is a request. It is a hand held out, trembling slightly, asking for permission to be seen. It is a state of constant, low-level anxiety, a fluctuating vital sign that depends entirely on how the person across from you chooses to behave. When you move through life in a state of hope, you are asking the environment to be kind to you, without providing any reason why it should. It is a weak way to live, a kind of emotional anemia where you are constantly waiting for a transfusion of validation from the outside world to feel whole.

Expectation, however, is an active alignment. It is the understanding that quality is your baseline, not a luxury you have to audition for. It functions like a regulatory system in the body; it maintains a constant internal environment regardless of the chaos outside. In the clinical world, we speak of homeostasis, the body's ability to remain stable even when the external temperature is freezing or boiling. Expectation is your emotional homeostasis. It is the set point of your life. If your set point is respect, your system will naturally reject anything that falls below that temperature. You won't even have to try to be strong; your system will automatically identify the disrespect as a foreign pathogen and move to neutralize it.

THE SELF-POSSESSED SHIELD

I've watched this play out in the smallest interactions, the kind we are taught to overlook because we've been told that noticing is a sign of being difficult or ungrateful. You see it when two women walk into the same space. One woman enters with the weight of home training pulling at her shoulders; she is careful not to be too much, difficult, and careful to be accommodating. She has been trained to believe that her value is tied to her adaptability, how easily she can be folded into the corners of someone else's convenience. She hopes for a good table, she hopes for prompt service, and she hopes to be treated with kindness. But because her energy is so available and penetrable, the world treats her with a casual dismissal. The staff senses the lack of structure in her presence before she even speaks. They see the way she shrinks to make room for others, the way she apologizes for taking up air, and they instinctively give her less because she has signaled she can survive on the margins.

Then, there is the woman who walks in with her frequency already set. She isn't loud. She isn't performing with confidence with a forced chin-tilt or an aggressive stride. She is simply settled. She doesn't hope for respect; she carries it as her primary vital sign. People respond to her not because she demanded it with words, but because her energy has already negotiated the terms of the engagement before she even sat down. Her posture is not a defensive wall; it is a clear filter.

This is the understanding that people treat you according to the energy you carry, not the credentials you hold. If your internal standard is high, the world finds it very difficult to offer you something low. It's as if her presence creates a localized atmosphere where only excellence is compatible. When you walk into a room expecting the best, you don't scan the room for threats; you scan for alignment. And because your eyes are only looking for what matches your frequency, the things that don't match eventually stop showing up in your line of sight.

Grooming & Attraction

THE SELF-POSSESSED SHIELD

We must speak about grooming without the shallow labels of vanity or the guilt of trying too hard that society uses to keep women in a state of disrepair. How a woman presents herself is not an aesthetic distraction; it is a form of internal regulation. It is how she maintains her own immunity against the world's attempt to silence her.

My nursing experience has always been flexible for me, mostly because I refused to let it be anything else. Even when it was my full-time career, I moved through it with a specific kind of autonomy. I chose roles that allowed me to inhabit my own skin, working when I wanted and stepping away when the environment started to feel like a cage. To me, that level of agency isn't just a perk; it's a vital sign.

The real test comes when you walk into a new facility and realize the people in charge are more interested in control than they are in competence. I have worked in places where management spent more energy policing the length of a woman's nails, the style of her hair, or the scent of her perfume than they did monitoring the quality of care in the wards. It's fascinating, really, in a dark way. These restrictions have almost nothing to do with professionalism and everything to do with trying to flatten a woman's identity until she's easier to manage. They want you to be a muted version of yourself so you'll be more compliant. In those situations, my response is: I simply do not go back.

Fortunately, the world of nursing is vast, which means no one is actually required to sit in a room where they are being diminished. But what always strikes me is how often people with a scarcity mindset will stay. I've watched women spend years complaining about the same suffocating conditions, the same rigid rules, the same lack of respect, yet they never leave. They talk as if the exit is a myth. They've been conditioned to believe that this is "just how it is," and so they stay until their spirit flatlines.

THE SELF-POSSESSED SHIELD

But the truth is that choice exists, but it only belongs to the woman who is actually willing to exercise it. The luxury of a boundary isn't just in saying no; it's in knowing you have the competence and the standards to walk through the door and find a room that actually matches your frequency. When an environment tries to force you into a shape that isn't yours, you don't need to argue or petition for a change of heart. You just withdraw your presence. You stop the bleeding by stopping the access. The truth is simple: it is difficult for the world to offer you mediocrity when you have stopped accepting it from yourself. Think of it as a clinical standard. A sterile environment in a hospital is not vibrant or ornamental; it is a requirement for safety. It is the barrier between life and infection. In the same way, your grooming and the way you present yourself create a sterile field where the bacteria of disrespect cannot easily grow. It forces people to wash their hands, metaphorically speaking, before they handle your time or your emotions. When you are polished, it's hard for you to get stained. You are signaling that you are a woman of high maintenance, not in the way the world mocks, but in the way a high-performance machine or a delicate instrument is maintained. You require precision because you operate with clarity.

How Self-respect Spurs your Confidence and Positions you for Attraction

This leads us to the reality that self-respect in action is often indistinguishable from confidence, but it is much more durable. Confidence is not static; it can fluctuate with a bad day, a harsh comment, or a social media feed. But self-respect is a structural integrity. It is the frame of the house. You cannot portray confidence if the foundation of self-respect is leaking. You can try to mask it with expensive clothes or strong perfumes, but the world senses the void. It is like a pulse that is fast but weak; it doesn't sustain the body, and it doesn't command the room.

THE SELF-POSSESSED SHIELD

True confidence is just self-respect in action. It is the daily choice to honor your own needs without writing a dissertation on why you deserve them. It shows up in the micro-decisions that build the muscle of your presence. It is the decision to leave a social circle that requires you to shrink to fit in, or the refusal to stay in a conversation that has turned into a critique of your character. It is the insistence on basic dignity in a professional meeting, even when you are the only one in the room who looks like you. These micro-decisions are the vital signs of a healthy life. If you ignore them, your spirit begins to flatline. These choices are like compound interest. They build a foundation that eventually becomes unshakeable. You don't have to "try" to be confident when you have a history of never betraying yourself. When you have spent years honoring your own peace, your rest, and your standards, confidence becomes your default state. You simply become a woman who doesn't know how to accept less, because "less" no longer matches your frequency. It feels as foreign to you as a mismatched blood type. If someone tries to give you energy that doesn't match yours, your system will naturally reject it without a fight.

We must examine why we were taught to fear this level of self-assurance. Why is a woman who knows her worth often viewed as a threat? Society often labels a woman with a high frequency as proud, difficult, or stuck up, especially when she refuses to participate in the drama of performing womanhood. They call it "forgetting your home training" when you stop making yourself small for the comfort of others. But we must be honest about what home training often was: It was a lesson in how to be a shock absorber for everyone else's bad behavior. When you decide to stop being a shock absorber, people will naturally be upset because they now have to feel the bumps in the road themselves. What they call pride, I call stabilization. What they call being difficult, I call having a regulatory filter. You are not being "mean" by having standards; you are being responsible for the energy you allow into your space. If you were a nurse and you allowed a contaminated needle into a sterile field, you wouldn't be kind, but negligent. The same applies to your life. Allowing disrespect into your space is not an act of grace; it is an act of negligence toward your own soul.

THE SELF-POSSESSED SHIELD

If your worth is measured by how much you can endure, the world will always give you more to carry. It will look at your strength and see a beast of burden rather than a woman of power. But if your worth is measured by what you choose to tolerate, the world will eventually stop trying to overload you. This is the shift from being a "good woman" in the patriarchal sense, a woman who is a receptacle for everyone else's needs, to being a woman who is the curator of her own life. It is the move to a stabilized existence. When you stabilize, the people who were used to your malleability will struggle. They will try to pull you back down to a lower frequency. They will use guilt, they will use tradition, and they will use the good woman's talk to try to make you feel selfish. But remember: selfishness is wanting others to live for you; self-respect is refusing to live for others at the expense of yourself. Your alignment is your primary responsibility. Without it, you have nothing to give that isn't tainted by resentment or exhaustion. When you are full, when you are polished, when you are settled in your expectation of excellence, you become a light that others can actually follow, rather than a door they simply walk through.

This is where your inner alignment finally meets the world's friction. It is the moment your new stability is tested by those who liked you better when you were easier to bend. It took me time to realize that the willingness to walk away is not a flare of anger, but proof that one can finally show respect to themselves. I mean, you can't claim to have a standard while staying in a space that consistently breaks it.

Most women struggle here because we have been socialized to view endurance as a spiritual currency. We are told that a woman's strength is found in her capacity to absorb, to wait, and to "fix" the broken dynamics around her. We are taught to rationalize poor treatment, to dress it up as a "misunderstanding" or a "lapse in judgment" on the part of the other person.

We spend hours in the laboratory of our own minds, trying to find the perfect combination of words that will finally make someone respect us. But respect is not a negotiation. It is a response to a standard. If you stay in a space where you are consistently offered less than what you expect, your expectation is no longer a standard; it is merely a suggestion.

You need to realize that the willingness to walk away is the ultimate luxury. It is the realization that your presence is a premium resource that requires a specific environment to remain stable. In the healthcare world, we understand that certain medications must be stored at precise temperatures to remain effective. If the environment becomes too hot or too cold, the medicine loses its potency; it becomes useless, or worse, toxic. You are no different. Your femininity, your peace, and your brilliance require an environment of respect to remain potent. When you stay in a toxic environment, you aren't being strong; you are allowing your potency to be neutralized.

I remember a time when this became real for me. I was in a professional space where my presence was being handled with a kind of casual, calculated dismissal. Because I was a Black woman, and because I showed up well-groomed and composed, there was an assumption that I was there to look good rather than do the work. Someone in charge tried to talk over me in a really condescending way, the kind of voice people use when they think they're better than you.

In a previous version of myself, the home-trained version, I might have felt the heat of embarrassment. I might have leaned forward to prove my intelligence, or worse, I might have shrunk back and swallowed my words to keep the peace. But on that day, I chose a different protocol. I simply stopped speaking. I allowed a heavy silence to fill the room. I didn't roll my eyes; I didn't sharpen my voice. I simply observed the behavior as if I were monitoring a patient's failing vitals. By refusing to chase the conversation or defend my right to be heard, I signaled that his behavior was beneath the frequency of the room I was inhabiting.

When you refuse to engage with a person's attempt to diminish you, you reclaim the power of the interaction. If you stay and fight for respect, you are still operating on their level. But when you are willing to simply withdraw your energy, to walk away from the table when respect is no longer being served, you move into a space they cannot reach. This is the click moment. It is the realization that the environment no longer matches your blood type. You don't need to be dramatic; you just need to be gone.

THE SELF-POSSESSED SHIELD

Walking away is often reframed by others as being too much or too difficult. We are told that we are throwing away relationships or opportunities because we have unrealistic expectations. But we must be clear: the only thing you are throwing away is the habit of self-betrayal. There is a profound grief that comes with this realization, especially when the person you have to walk away from is someone you once hoped would see you. But hope, as we discussed, is not a strategy for a well-lived life. You cannot hope a person will treat you better; you can only decide what you will no longer tolerate. This willingness to leave is what gives your "yes" its value. If your no has no consequences, then your yes has no meaning. We see this in the way we handle our time and our emotions. If you tell someone that you require punctuality, but you wait for them for an hour every time they are late, you are not teaching them to respect you; you are teaching them that your time is a discount commodity. But the woman who waits ten minutes and then leaves to go about her day, not out of spite, but out of a standard for her own life, is a woman who is teaching the world her frequency. She does not need to shout. Her absence speaks

THE SELF-POSSESSED SHIELD

with such clarity that words can never achieve.

This is the compound effect of self-respect. Every time you walk away from a situation that dims you, you are performing a life-saving procedure on your own soul. You are clearing the pathogens. You are ensuring that your internal environment remains sterile and safe. Over time, this becomes automatic. You begin to sense the drop in the room's energy long before a word is spoken. You develop an immunity to the good-woman-guilt. You realize that you are not difficult for wanting a life that is high-quality; you are simply a woman who has stopped accepting the scraps that society tells you are a feast. We must treat our peace with the same urgency we treat a vital organ. You would not negotiate with an infection that was trying to stop your heart. You would move to eliminate it with precision. Why, then, do we negotiate with relationships, jobs, or social expectations that are trying to stop our peace? The "Self-Possessed Shield" is not a wall you build to keep the world out; it is the standard you carry that determines what is allowed to stay in. When you are willing to walk away, you aren't losing anything. You are finally making room for the excellence you actually deserve.

CHAPTER 6
The Daily Practice of Walking "Shoulders-high"

There is a common, almost lazy assumption that confidence is a fixed trait, something you are either gifted with at birth or denied by some cosmic oversight. We look at women who move through the world with an unshakeable presence and assume they possess a magical kind of self-assurance that we lack. But the truth is much more grounded: confidence is a daily practice. It is not a grand, cinematic event; it is built in the smallest, most mundane moments of your life. It is a muscle that either grows because you use it or gets weak because you don't.

Confidence is built in the morning, in that space between your alarm and your first step out the door, when you decide whether to tend to yourself or rush out into the world as an afterthought. It is built when you choose the restaurant, the hotel, or the circle of friends that actually matches your standard, even when the easier, more manageable option is to just settle.

THE SELF-POSSESSED SHIELD

The women who appear most confident are not special; they are simply women who have practiced choosing themselves so many times that it has become second nature. They have reached a point where self-betrayal is no longer an option because they have spent years perfecting the art of staying true to their own needs.

We need to talk about the friction between our culture and the way the world often tries to shame women for caring about how they look. In many places, investing heavily in your appearance is dismissed as shallow or vain. People act like, if you care about your hair, your skin, or your clothes, you must not have much going on in your head. Western feminism has often looked at this level of self-presentation as a burden, as if we are performing for an audience that doesn't deserve our time. But this misses the fundamental wisdom that many of us carry in our bones: how you present yourself is how you honor yourself. In the culture I was raised in, and in many others, wanting the best in a modest setting was always framed as pride or impracticality. There is a deep, ancestral understanding that your presentation is your primary tool for navigating the world.

THE SELF-POSSESSED SHIELD

When a Nigerian woman prioritizes her grooming and her overall presence, she isn't doing it for a man or for status; she is doing it because she knows that when you feel beautiful, you move through the world differently. Your gait changes. Your voice carries more weight. You inhabit your space with a voice that doesn't need to be explained or defended. I've always found it funny how people try to label self-care as frivolous. It ignores the fact that looking in the mirror and feeling proud of the woman staring back is a way of stabilizing your own mind. When you take the time to put yourself together, you are telling your own heart that you are worth the effort. You are signaling to your own system that you are a priority, even when the rest of the world is trying to put you at the bottom of the list. It is the realization that your body is not just something to be used for work; it is a home that deserves to be tended to with care. If you don't care for the home you live in, how can you expect anyone else to walk in and treat it with respect? This is where the practice starts. It starts with the decision that you will not look like what you've been through, no matter how heavy the day feels. People with a scarcity mindset will tell you that you're doing too much, but that's usually because they've been conditioned to survive on too little.

True confidence is about consistency. I've noticed that a lot of women are taught to switch their standards on and off depending on who is watching. They are bold at work but passive at home. They dress up for a big wedding but allow themselves to look completely drained at the grocery store or the gym. But this situational confidence is just a mask, and people can sense when it isn't real. You should not have different versions of yourself for different price points.

You don't "dress down" your energy just because the setting is modest. Whether I am at a high-stakes meeting or just heading to the gym, I maintain my standard. That's why I'll go to the gym with a bit of makeup and a neat outfit, not because I'm looking for attention, but because I am a woman who values herself every single hour of the day. When you consistently behave like a woman who expects quality, people instinctively feel that. You don't even have to ask for good service; you expect it, and that expectation sets the tone for every person who walks into your space.

THE SELF-POSSESSED SHIELD

Energy speaks much louder than a price tag. People respond to the stability you carry inside, not the location you happen to be standing in. If you are in a budget setting but you still carry yourself with self-respect, you will find that the world adjusts to you. This is about more than just clothes; it's about the "texture" of how you exist. We are intuitive beings. We can feel when a boundary has been crossed or when an environment is beneath us long before our brains have a word for it.

The practice of walking "shoulders-high" is the practice of honoring those signals. If a space feels cheap, rushed, or disrespectful, you have to be willing to acknowledge that feeling rather than suppressing it to be "nice." If you stay in an environment that offends your spirit, you are telling yourself that your peace is a discount commodity that can be traded for someone else's convenience.

This daily accumulation of choices works like compound interest. Each time you wake up a little earlier to groom yourself, even when you're tired, you are adding to your foundation. Each time you speak up when service is poor, not with anger, but with the clarity of someone who knows what they deserve, you are making yourself stronger. When you walk away from friendships that leave you feeling drained, even when being alone feels scary, you are protecting your own life. These choices might seem small, but they build a foundation that nobody can shake. You reach a point where self-betrayal feels like a language you don't speak anymore. You become a woman who cannot be rushed or pressured, because you have a long history of never letting yourself down.

THE SELF-POSSESSED SHIELD

We have to be careful about the "just manage" trap. In Nigeria, where I come from, we hear it all the time, just manage, don't be too difficult. It's a way of training women to accept less while feeling guilty for wanting more. But there is a massive difference between being entitled and having a standard. Entitlement is wanting something for nothing; a standard is knowing what you bring to the table and refusing to sit where that value isn't recognized. When you walk "shoulders-high," you are signaling that you are the curator of your own life. You are the one who decides who gets access to your energy. You stop being a shock absorber for other people's chaos. When you stop being available for everyone else's bad behavior, they will call you proud. Let them. That discomfort they feel is just the friction of your new boundaries hitting their old expectations. Walking with your shoulders high is an act of rebellion in a world that wants you to stay small and apologetic. It's about the posture of your heart. It's about the way you handle your time, the way you answer the phone, and the way you allow people to speak to you. It's a million tiny "nos" to mediocrity so that you can say a big "yes" to the life you actually want. Real confidence is how you treat yourself when you're alone, and no one is there to applaud you.

Once you start living this way, you realize that the world has no choice but to respond to the woman you've finally decided to be. You stop asking for permission to occupy space. You just occupy it. If you don't believe you deserve great treatment, you won't expect it, and you certainly won't get it. You have to believe you are the best thing in the room before the room will ever agree with you.

How Can One Do This Practically?

To show exactly how these bricks of self-respect are laid, we have to look at the anatomy of a week lived with the shoulders high. It isn't enough to understand the theory in the safety of a book; you have to see the protocol in action when the world is rushing you, when your body is tired, and when the cultural pressure to "just manage" starts to feel like a physical weight on your chest.

THE SELF-POSSESSED SHIELD

Confidence is rarely forged in the moments when everything is going perfectly; it is forged in the mundane decisions you make when no one is watching and there is no audience to applaud your standards. It is about what happens in the dark, in the early hours, and in the budget spaces where society expects you to lower your guard and accept less. It is easy to be polished when you are being celebrated; it is much harder to be polished when you are simply existing in the thick of a stressful Tuesday.

Think of a typical Monday morning. For most people, this is a state of emergency, a frantic, disorganized race to beat the clock where grooming is rushed, and the self is treated like an annoying afterthought. They wake up to a loud alarm, scroll through their phones to see what the world wants from them, and then scramble to get out the door. But for the woman committed to her own frequency, this is the first battle of the day, and it is won before she ever speaks to another soul.

THE SELF-POSSESSED SHIELD

Even if the stress of school or work is high, you choose the ritual of putting yourself together. You don't see this as a chore. You see it as the way you show love to yourself. You stand before the mirror, and you press your clothes with a certain kind of attention. You sweep your hair into a neat, disciplined bun. You aren't doing this for a man or for a status symbol; you are doing it because you care about yourself as a person and as a lady.

There is a psychological shift that happens when you refuse to "look like what you've been through." When you stand in that mirror, even when you've had a rough night or a stressful week, and you choose to present yourself with excellence, you are telling your heart that its peace is non-negotiable. You are signalling to your own nervous system that you are in control, even if the world outside is in a state of chaos.

THE SELF-POSSESSED SHIELD

My nursing classmates used to be baffled by this. They would look at me, well-groomed while they were disheveled and frantic, and ask, "How long does it take you to get ready?" The question always confused me because it implied that taking care of yourself was an extra burden rather than the foundation of your day. They saw the time I spent on myself as something I was losing, but I saw it as the very thing that kept me from losing myself in the madness of the ward. By Tuesday, you might find yourself in an environment that is designed to drain you. In many professional circles, especially in healthcare, looking haggard is almost seen as a badge of competence. There is this silent, annoying curriculum that suggests if you look tired, you must be working hard, and if you look put-together, you aren't serious. You will meet people who assume you aren't competent simply because you look pretty or well-groomed.

THE SELF-POSSESSED SHIELD

They will try to use your appearance as a reason to dismiss your intelligence. In those moments, you don't shrink. You don't apologize for the effort you put into yourself. You realize that their negative reaction has nothing to do with you and everything to do with their own low self-esteem or the fact that they have made their professional title their entire identity. You stay settled in your choice, knowing that your patients and clients actually feel a positive energy when they are cared for by someone who clearly respects themselves. Mid-week is usually when the "Environmental Alignment Principle" gets tested in the most mundane ways. You might be heading to the gym or stopping by a local shop, and the temptation to match the "low energy" of a budget room is strong. Society tells us that we only need to try when it's a special occasion. But for the woman with high standards, every day is an occasion. You go to the gym with a bit of makeup and a neat outfit because you come from a culture where women take pride in putting themselves together. You aren't there for male attention; you are there because you know that when you look good, you tend to feel good. And as a woman, feeling good radiates a positive aura that people around you can feel and enjoy.

This is where you see the "Echo Effect" in real time. Because you consistently behave like a woman who values herself, people instinctively give you better service. You don't have to ask for quality; you expect it. It's as if your presence forces the people around you to wash their hands, metaphorically speaking, before they handle your time.

You notice that even in the most average settings, you are treated with a level of care that others aren't receiving. It isn't because you are special; it's because your standard doesn't shift based on the location. You don't adapt to the environment; you let the environment rise to you. This consistency is what makes you magnetic. When people see that your standard is not a performance for them, but a requirement for yourself, they stop trying to offer you mediocrity.

THE SELF-POSSESSED SHIELD

By Thursday, the "just manage" trap often appears in your personal life. This is perhaps the hardest brick to lay. In the culture I was raised in, we believe that endurance is a virtue, that we must hold onto relationships, especially family, at all costs. We hear phrases like "just manage," and we are taught to stay loyal even when it hurts us. But this is where you must be firm.

You have to learn that peace of mind is priceless and that not everyone deserves access to you. Setting a boundary doesn't make you disrespectful, and choosing your own sanity doesn't make you ungrateful. You have to be okay with being labeled "problematic" or "too foreign" by people who benefited from you having no boundaries. If someone drains you, if they force you to sacrifice your mental well-being just to keep the relationship alive, they have already shown you that they do not value your presence.

THE SELF-POSSESSED SHIELD

Cutting people off isn't about being angry; it's about clarity. It's about choosing a life where your heart is protected. You are allowed to outgrow people, even if they share your last name. Loyalty should never feel like self-betrayal, and you are allowed to protect the life you are building, even if others whisper that you've changed.

There is a specific kind of grief that comes with this realization, but it is the necessary price of a life lived with integrity. You cannot build a sanctuary while you are still allowing people to trample through the hallways with dirty shoes. You have to be the one to decide when the house is closed to those who don't know how to respect it.

As the week comes to a close, you might find yourself in a space where your value is being questioned based on your ethnicity. I have traveled extensively, and one thing I've noticed is that people will often try to give a Black woman the "shorter end of the stick." They assume you won't notice or that you'll be too "home-trained" to say anything. In the past, you might have swallowed your words to keep the peace.

THE SELF-POSSESSED SHIELD

Now, you advocate for yourself. You let it be known that you will not accept anything less than the best. You realize that if you don't believe you deserve great treatment, you won't expect it, and if you don't expect it, you'll never demand it. You advocate for yourself because you know that high-quality service is not just about the function of what is done, but the texture of how it feels. If the texture is wrong, you walk away.

This accumulation of small, daily choices is how you build a life that no one can destabilize. It is a million tiny "nos" to mediocrity. You start by owning your morning, refusing to rush for a world that doesn't care about your peace. You audit your consistency, making sure you are the same woman in the grocery store as you are in the gala.

THE SELF-POSSESSED SHIELD

You listen to your sensory signals, that feeling in your gut that tells you when a boundary is being nudged. You reject the "just manage" culture that wants you to be a beast of burden. And finally, you become okay with the silence that follows when you walk away from chaos. This is not about being cold; it is about being contained. It is about recognizing that your energy is your most precious currency, and you must be the one to decide who is worthy of the investment.

When you live this way, you aren't just becoming confident; you are inhabiting your own value. You stop being a door people walk through and start being a sanctuary they have to be invited into. You realize that your presence is the most valuable thing you own. Once you're settled into this frequency, the world stops trying to offer you scraps because it realizes you are no longer a woman who knows how to eat them.

THE SELF-POSSESSED SHIELD

You walk with your shoulders high, not to look down on others, but to ensure your eyes are always fixed on the excellence you deserve. It is a long game, a slow build, but the result is a life that is entirely your own. You no longer need to look for validation on the outside because you have built a foundation on the inside that is so sturdy, it doesn't need a witness to be real.

CHAPTER 7
Luxury Is a Behavior, Not a Price Tag

There is a kind of social conditioning that tries to convince us that our right to excellence is tied to our financial footprint. We are taught to believe that if we aren't paying a premium, we have no business expecting a premium experience. This lie is designed to keep women in a state of apology, essentially telling us that our dignity is a variable that fluctuates with our bank balance. But the truth is far more liberating: luxury is a behavior, not a price tag. It is a way of inhabiting your space that has nothing to do with the market value of the floor you are standing on.

THE SELF-POSSESSED SHIELD

You do not need to wait for a specific tax bracket to decide that your life is worth the effort of precision. We have been sold a version of high standards that is consumer-based, meaning we think we have to buy our way into being respected. We think that if we are in a place where the soup is cheap, or the chairs are plastic, we have to lower our internal temperature to match the room. This is the first lie we have to dismantle. Your value as a woman is the only luxury that actually matters in any room, and that value is a constant. It does not go up when you enter a boutique, and it does not go down when you enter a local market.

When you look at the way the world is structured, you see a silent, cultural contract that tries to dictate who is allowed to be particular. Society agrees that if you are spending ten thousand dollars, you are allowed to be firm, you are allowed to ask for things to be done correctly, and you are allowed to expect a certain level of deference. But if you are spending ten dollars, that same society expects you to be grateful, and invisible. They want you to trade your standards for a discount.

THE SELF-POSSESSED SHIELD

This is why many women feel a strange sense of guilt or shame when they maintain their poise in a budget environment. They feel like they are being too much because the surroundings are too little. But this is a trap. If your requirement for dignity is a volume knob that you turn down based on the price point of the service, then you aren't actually a person of high standards; you are just a consumer of them. A consumer waits for the environment to provide the quality, but a woman of substance brings the quality with her. She understands that she is the source of the value, not the building she is standing in.

Dismantling this lie requires us to understand that "expensive" is a marketing term, but excellence is a character trait. You can buy something expensive, but you cannot buy excellence; you have to inhabit it. I have seen women who have all the money in the world but no weight to their presence. They walk into high-end spaces and practically beg the staff to notice them because they don't feel they belong there without the label. Their standards are a performance.

Then, I have seen women who understand that luxury is a behavior. These are the women who carry themselves with clarity regardless of where they are. They understand that their time, their body, and their conversation are premium resources. When you live with this realization, you stop waiting for a specific environment to permit you to be great. You don't code-switch your self-respect. You don't decide to be polished only when you're at a high-end gala and then allow yourself to be dismissed or disheveled when you're at the grocery store.

We have to talk about the "just manage" trap again, but through the lens of economics. In the culture I was raised in, we are often told that wanting the best in a modest setting is a sign of pride or being unrealistic. People will say, "Why are you acting like this? It's just a local shop." This is a form of gaslighting. It is designed to make you feel like you are being difficult for wanting things to be done correctly. But the truth is that your standards are your internal regulatory system.

THE SELF-POSSESSED SHIELD

They are the fence you build around your life. If you allow people to trample over that fence just because the setting is humble, you are training your spirit to accept mediocrity as a way of life. Luxury is the refusal to accept scraps, no matter how much they cost. It is the understanding that your peace and your comfort are not for sale. If you allow yourself to accept the shorter end of the stick because you feel you haven't paid enough for the long one, you are telling yourself that you are only worthy of respect when you can afford it.

This internal shift is the most important part of the "shoulders-high" journey. It is the realization that your dignity is not a commodity that fluctuates with the stock market. It is a non-negotiable requirement of your existence. When you stop looking at luxury as something you buy and start looking at it as something you are, everything changes. You stop asking for permission to be excellent. You stop apologizing for being particular about your time and your surroundings.

You begin to understand that you don't need a promotion, a windfall, or a designer bag to live a high-quality life. You can start today by refusing to trade your self-respect for a discount. You can start by treating your own presence as the most expensive thing in the room. This is not about being entitled; it is about being disciplined. Entitlement is wanting something for nothing; a standard is knowing what you bring to the table and refusing to sit where that value isn't recognized.

We also have to dismantle the idea that being refined or polished is a performance for other people. Many women think that if they aren't in a place where people will appreciate their grooming or their tone, then there is no point in maintaining it. They think, "Why should I dress up to go to the pharmacy? No one important will see me." This is the core of the problem. If your standards are for other people, then you are a performer.

But if your standards are for you, then you are a queen. A queen does not stop being a queen because she is walking through a village; she is a queen because of how she handles herself, not because of the throne she sits on. When you maintain your standards when no one is watching, you are telling yourself that you are the most important person in your world. You are building a foundation of self-respect that is sturdy enough to withstand any setting. This consistency is what makes a woman magnetic. People can sense when your standards are not a performance. They can feel that your requirement for excellence is an internal climate that you carry with you. When you walk into a budget space with that frequency, you aren't reacting to the furniture; you are setting the tone for everyone who interacts with you. You'll find that when you move with this level of internal stabilization, the world begins to offer you "luxury" treatment even in the most average settings. It's as if your energy makes anything less than excellence feel incompatible. This is the ultimate liberation. It removes the barrier between who you are and the quality of life you deserve to lead right now. You stop waiting for one day, and you start living as that woman today. You realize that your value is not a moving target tied to a bank statement. You are the source, and the world is just the mirror.

I want you to think about the spaces you've occupied where you felt you had to shrink because you didn't want to seem too demanding. Maybe it was a local clinic where the wait was long, and the staff was rude, and you sat there in silence, accepting the disrespect because it was free or cheap. Or maybe it was a basic restaurant where the table was dirty, but you didn't say anything because you didn't want to be that person.

Every time you do that, you are signing a contract that says your dignity is tied to the price tag. You are telling yourself that your peace is worth less than the money you saved. But the woman who understands luxury as a behavior knows that her peace is priceless. She isn't loud or aggressive; she is simply firm. She doesn't negotiate for basic respect. If the texture of the environment is wrong, she either advocates for a change or she withdraws her presence. She doesn't "just manage."

THE SELF-POSSESSED SHIELD

This behavior is a service to your own nervous system. When you live in a state of apology, constantly shrinking to fit into mediocre spaces, you are living in a state of low-level stress. You are constantly telling yourself that you don't matter. But when you maintain your frequency, when you refuse to lower your head or mumble your words just because the setting is modest, you are keeping yourself stabilized. You are protecting your own energy. You are saying to the world, "I am here, and I am a woman of quality."

The Pillars Of The Luxury Effect

The physical manifestation of your internal standards is built on four pillars: posture, tone, grooming, and aura. These are not just aesthetic choices; they are sensory negotiators. They communicate to every person in the room, from the CEO to the janitor, exactly how you expect to be handled. In a budget space, where people are often treated like numbers or inconveniences, these four pillars act as a barrier against the casual disrespect that society often throws at anyone who isn't spending a fortune. You have to understand that your body is constantly speaking on your behalf, and if you aren't intentional about what it's saying, the world will fill in the blanks with its own mediocre assumptions.

THE SELF-POSSESSED SHIELD

Posture is the first thing people notice, and it is the most immediate way to signal that you are a woman of high maintenance. It isn't about being stiff or appearing unapproachable; it is about alignment. When you slouch, you are literally shrinking your presence. You are telling the room that you are trying to take up as little space as possible, which is an invitation for people to overlook you or rush you. But when you stand with your shoulders back and your chin parallel to the floor, you are inhabiting your full height. You are signaling that you are present and actively paying attention. This is particularly powerful in crowded, disorganized environments like a busy clinic or a government office. While everyone else is hunched over their phones in a state of defeated waiting, your posture sets you apart. It says that your time is still valuable, even if the system is slow. It creates a no-fly zone around your person that forces people to approach you with a bit more intentionality.

THE SELF-POSSESSED SHIELD

The second pillar is your tone. There is a specific kind of frequency that I call the "Settled Voice." Most people, when they are in a budget space and they want something, either speak with a timid, apologetic mumble or they lean into an aggressive, loud demand. Both of these come from a place of insecurity. The mumble says, "I don't think I deserve this," and the shout says, "I'm afraid you won't give it to me." A woman who understands luxury as a behavior speaks with the utmost clarity and confidence. She doesn't need to raise her voice to be heard because the weight of her words comes from her internal stabilization. When you speak slowly and clearly, without the frantic filler words, you are saying that you expect to be understood and obeyed. It is a firm frequency that cuts through the noise of a chaotic environment. It tells the clerk or the manager that you are not someone who can be easily dismissed with a scripted excuse.

THE SELF-POSSESSED SHIELD

Then there is grooming. We have touched on this before, but it bears a deeper look in the context of the luxury effect. Your grooming is your visual resume. It is the texture of your presence. In a budget space, society expects you to look casual or perhaps even a bit neglected, because the assumption is that if you had the money to look better, you wouldn't be there. This is a classic trap that you must refuse to fall into. When you show up well-groomed, with neat hair, a polished appearance, and clothes that fit you well, you are performing an act of self-honor. You are telling the world that your standards for yourself do not change based on the price of the room. This creates a psychological friction in the minds of those serving you. They see a woman who clearly values herself, and it becomes very difficult for them to offer her a low-value experience. Your grooming acts as a filter; it filters out the lazy, good enough attitude that is so common in modest settings.

Finally, there is your aura. This is the hardest one to define, but it is the most potent. Your aura is the energy you leave behind in a room. It is the "scent" of your standards. It is built on the consistency of the first three pillars. When you are aligned in your posture, settled in your tone, and polished in your grooming, you develop a frequency of "containment." You don't leak energy. You don't look around frantically for approval. You are settled in your own skin.

This containment is what people mean when they say a woman is "expensive." It isn't about her jewelry; it's about the fact that she seems to be the owner of her own peace. In a budget space, where energy is often scattered and frantic, a contained woman is a luxury. People are naturally drawn to that stability, and they will often go out of their way to protect it.

THE SELF-POSSESSED SHIELD

Carrying this energy into a budget space requires a specific kind of mental discipline. You have to resist the urge to "dress down" your personality to fit the surroundings. I've seen women who are bold and articulate in a high-end setting, but the moment they walk into a local market, they start using slang they don't normally use, or they adopt a passive, humble persona. They think they are being relatable, but they are actually betraying their own excellence. You should be the same woman everywhere. You don't need to be arrogant, but you must be consistent.

If you are a woman who values precision, then you should expect precision in the grocery store just as much as in the boardroom. If you are a woman who values politeness, then you should require it from the person selling you bread just as much as from the person selling you a car. This consistency is what builds the "luxury" effect. It proves that your standards are a part of your identity, not a tool you use for social climbing.

We must also talk about the "Texture of Service." High-quality service is not just about getting what you ask for; it is about how the interaction feels. In budget spaces, the function is usually there: you get your coffee, you get your receipt, you get your seat, but the texture is often rough. It's rushed, it's cold, or it's indifferent. Most people accept this because they think, "Well, it was cheap, what do you expect?" But a woman who walks with her shoulders high knows that her dignity has no discount. She pays attention to the texture.

If a clerk is being dismissive or if the environment is unnecessarily chaotic, she doesn't manage. She uses her tone and her posture to reset the interaction. She might say, "I'd appreciate it if we could slow down for a moment," or "I'm sure we can find a cleaner space to handle this." She isn't being a "Karen"; she is being a curator. She is advocating for a higher texture of existence.

THE SELF-POSSESSED SHIELD

Now to the most important "luxury behavior" of all: the willingness to walk away. The ultimate sign of high standards is not just expecting the best, but refusing to stay where the best isn't possible. If you are in a space where the respect texture is fundamentally broken, and your attempts to reset it are ignored, you must have the courage to withdraw your presence. It doesn't matter if it's a cheap place or an expensive one.

If the environment requires you to shrink or to accept disrespect, it is an environment that is beneath you. Your presence is a premium resource, and you should never spend it in a place that treats it like a discount commodity. The power to say, "This isn't for me," and walk out with your head held high is the ultimate luxury. It shows that you value your peace more than the convenience of the transaction.

THE SELF-POSSESSED SHIELD

There is a social friction that comes with living this way. People who have agreed to live in mediocrity will often feel triggered by your standards. They will call you proud, difficult, or too much. They will try to shame you, and you have to be okay with that. Their discomfort is a sign that your light is shining on their laziness. You aren't being mean; you are being disciplined. You are treating your life with the same surgical precision you'd want from a doctor. You wouldn't want a doctor who just manages with a dirty scalpel, so why would you want a life that manages with dirty energy? Your standards are a form of health. They keep your spirit stabilized and your mind clear.

Luxury is the freedom to be excellent anywhere, at any time, under any circumstances. It is the firm certainty that you deserve the best, not because you paid for it, but because you are it. It is the refusal to let a price tag dictate your posture or your tone. When you live this way, you realize that you have all the power. You don't need a boutique to tell you who you are.

THE SELF-POSSESSED SHIELD

You don't need a five-star hotel to tell you how you should be handled. You are the one who decides. You are the curator. You are the lady. And in a world that is constantly trying to make you settle for less, choosing to be your own luxury is the most powerful act of rebellion you can perform. It is the foundation of a life lived with shoulders high, and it is a gift that only you can give to yourself.

Your standards are not a burden; they are your beauty. They are the way you honor the woman you have become. And once you stop apologizing for them, you will realize that the world has no choice but to start honoring them, too. This is not a dream for the future; it is a reality for right now. You are the premium resource.

But understanding the "why" of this internal shift is only the first step; the real transformation happens when you begin to master the physical language of that worth. It is in the way you occupy space, the way you modulate your voice in a crowded room, and the way you use your grooming as a protective shield. This is where the internal frequency meets the external world, turning the concept of luxury into a tangible, unshakeable reality that people can feel before you even open your mouth.

CHAPTER 8
Prioritizing Yourself

When we talk about the architecture of a woman's life, we often spend a great deal of time discussing what she builds for others and almost no time discussing the perimeter she must build for herself. We are conditioned to believe that our primary role is to be a sanctuary for everyone else's storms, a place where brothers, parents, and partners can come to shed their burdens while we buckle under the weight. This is the cultural curriculum of the good woman, a woman who is essentially an open field, with no fences and no gates, available for anyone to trample through at any hour of the day. But a life without a perimeter is not a life lived with the shoulders high; it is a life lived in a state of constant occupation.

To truly inhabit your own power, you have to move past the fear of being difficult and embrace the necessity of being guarded. You have to realize that your energy is not a public utility; it is a private, premium resource that requires a strict protocol for access. This

THE SELF-POSSESSED SHIELD

realization usually begins with the "Oxygen Mask Principle," a concept we often pay lip service to but rarely implement. In a crisis, the instruction is clear because the stakes are visible: you cannot help anyone else if you are unconscious. Yet, in our personal lives, we try to perform miracles while we are emotionally and spiritually suffocating. We tell ourselves that we are being selfless, but what we are actually doing is practicing self-betrayal. When you nurture others at the direct expense of your own peace, you aren't offering them a gift; you are offering them a sacrifice. And sacrifice, over time, always curdles into resentment. You cannot pour from an empty vessel, and even if you manage to scrape the bottom to find a few drops for someone else, those drops will be poisoned by the bitterness of your own depletion.

Across every major health and labor metric, women give more and pay for it physically over time. Women perform 60–75% of all unpaid caregiving labor, even when working full-time, and mothers spend significantly more hours per week on childcare and household management than fathers. As a result, women caregivers are 30–40% more likely to develop cardiovascular disease, twice as likely to suffer from depression and anxiety, and account for nearly 80% of all autoimmune disease diagnoses, including lupus, rheumatoid arthritis, and multiple sclerosis conditions strongly linked to chronic stress and immune dysregulation. Women also experience higher rates of chronic fatigue, fibromyalgia 2-9× more than men, sleep disorders, and inflammatory illness, while delaying their own medical care at higher rates due to prioritizing family needs. Though women live longer than men, they spend more total years in poor health, disability, and pain, revealing a paradox where longevity is achieved at the expense of vitality.

Women carry the weight of care in ways their bodies eventually record. Globally and in the U.S., women perform the majority of unpaid caregiving raising children, tending to households, and caring for aging relatives often while neglecting their own rest and recovery. Medically, this chronic overextension shows consequences: women caregivers have up to a 35% higher risk of cardiovascular disease, are twice as likely to experience depression and anxiety, and account for nearly 80% of autoimmune disease diagnoses, conditions strongly linked to prolonged stress and immune dysregulation. Though women live longer than men, they spend more years in chronic illness and disability, revealing a healthspan shortened not by weakness, but by prolonged self-sacrifice. What is praised socially as devotion often manifests biologically as inflammation, fatigue, and disease.

The True Cost of Infinite Accessibility

The problem with being a woman who is always there is that people eventually stop seeing you as a human being and start seeing you as a function. You become a tool, a fixer, a listener, a bank, a shock absorber. The cost of this infinite accessibility is the slow erosion of your own internal landscape. When your schedule is dictated by other people's emergencies and your emotional state is a reflection of their chaos, you have effectively handed over the keys to your life. This depletion doesn't happen in a single, dramatic moment; it happens in a thousand small "yeses" that should have been "nos." It happens every time you pick up the phone for a relative who only calls to dump their drama on you. It happens every time you "just manage" a

THE SELF-POSSESSED SHIELD

situation that actually requires you to walk away.

Resentment is the sensory signal that your cup is not just empty, but leaking. It is that tightening in your chest when a certain name pops up on your screen, or that feeling of being drained before the day has even begun. Most women are taught to suppress this feeling, to pray it away, or to be more patient. But patience with a boundary violator is just an invitation for further violation. To exude feminine energy and a settled confidence, you have to stop apologizing for your limits. You have to understand that your no is a complete sentence. Protecting your well-being will inevitably mean disappointing people who have grown accustomed to your lack of boundaries. Their disappointment is not your burden to carry; it is simply the sound of them hitting a wall that should have been built years ago.

Care without boundaries becomes pathology, giving without restoration becomes disease, and love without limits becomes depletion. The illnesses women develop are not random, they are patterned responses to prolonged self-sacrifice.

Even though statistics consistently show that women live longer, they spend more total years in poor health, marked by higher rates of disability, chronic pain, and polypharmacy. In other words, women may gain longevity but often at a significant physical cost.

Prolonged stress, particularly from caregiving and emotional labor, is closely associated with a higher prevalence of the following conditions among women:

- Metabolic Disorders (Obesity, Type 2 Diabetes):

Mothers, especially those carrying multiple caregiving roles often experience limited time for physical activity, disrupted sleep, and stress-driven eating patterns. Chronic cortisol elevation contributes to insulin resistance, central adiposity, and metabolic syndrome.

- Depression & Anxiety Disorders:

Women are diagnosed with major depressive and generalized anxiety disorders at roughly twice the rate of men. Female caregivers report two to three times higher rates of depression than their male counterparts, with mothers and sandwich-generation women carrying the highest burden.

People believe that marriage extends men's lives because women give. Women's lives, on the other hand, are shortened when they give too much. This is because women are socialized to pour until they are empty and then praised for the sacrifice.

Navigating the Cultural Shame of the "Proud" Daughter

In the Nigerian context, the transition from a people-pleaser to a woman with a perimeter is often met with fierce resistance. We come from a culture where "blood is blood" is used as a weapon to justify all manner of emotional and financial abuse. If you decide to prioritize your own peace over a toxic family dynamic, you will be met with a specific vocabulary of shame. They will call you proud. They will say you have become too foreign for the realities of home. They will claim you are being disrespectful, not because you have insulted them, but because you have dared to stop being an easy target for their dysfunction. You must realize that these labels are nothing more than tools of manipulation. They are the screams of people who have lost their free access to your labor and your light.

There is a specific kind of strength required to be too foreign for chaos. It means you have outgrown the curriculum of endurance. You have decided that your life is not a beast of burden and that your shoulders were not designed to carry the weight of grown adults who refuse to carry their own. When they call you proud, take it as a sign that your boundaries are working. It means you have successfully signaled that you are a woman of high maintenance, one who maintains her own mental health with the same attention she gives to her grooming. You are not being cold; you are being contained. You are finally deciding that your sanctuary is not a public park, and not everyone is invited to the picnic.

Setting boundaries with people who share your history requires a new kind of vocabulary. You cannot use the old, apologetic language and expect a different result. You have to move away from explaining yourself, because explanations are often treated as negotiations. When you explain why you can't do something, you are giving a boundary violator the information they need to dismantle your reasoning. Instead, you must use the language of finality. "I am not available for this right now," or "That doesn't work for me," or "I am no longer willing to discuss this topic." These are firm, settled statements that don't leave room for a counteroffer. It feels uncomfortable at first, like wearing a new pair of shoes that are a bit too stiff, but eventually, this clarity becomes your natural gait.

Creating distance from loved ones is often the most painful part of the shoulders-high journey, but it is sometimes the only way to save yourself. This isn't about being cutthroat; it's about the realization that some people are only compatible with the versions of you that were willing to suffer. As you grow and evolve, you will find that certain relationships can only survive if you stay small. When you start to expand, the friction becomes unbearable. You might have to step back from a childhood friend who thrives on drama, or a sibling who views your success as their personal ATM. This distance isn't a punishment you are inflicting on them; it is a protective measure for the life you are building. It is the understanding that you cannot build a skyscraper on a foundation of shifting sand.

Removing access from someone you love is an act of grief. You have to mourn the relationship you wish you had while acknowledging the reality of the one you actually have. This is the hardest part of self-prioritization: the fact that you can love someone and still recognize that they cannot be in your inner circle. You can wish them well from across the fence. You can pray for them from a distance. But you must refuse to let their dysfunction become your daily bread. This mourning process is necessary because it honors the history you shared without allowing that history to hold your future hostage. You are allowed to protect the woman you are becoming, even if it means leaving behind the people who only loved the woman you used to be.

Walking away from a toxic dynamic is like clearing a sterile field. Initially, it feels empty, and that silence can be terrifying for a woman who has spent her whole life managing noise. But in that silence, you find your own frequency again. You begin to see what your life looks like when it isn't a reaction to someone else's crisis.

THE SELF-POSSESSED SHIELD

You find that your aura becomes brighter, your tone becomes more settled, and your shoulders naturally rise because they are no longer braced for an impact. Life after a necessary exit is not a life of loneliness; it is a life of curated peace. You find that you have more energy for the people who actually respect your perimeter, and more importantly, you have more energy for yourself.

Filling the Vessel to Overflow

To exude true feminine energy, you must understand that your power lies in your containment. A woman who is always leaking energy, always rushing to please, and always over-extending herself is a woman whose frequency is scattered. But a woman who fills her own cup first, who prioritizes her rest, her grooming, her solitude, and her joy, becomes a magnetic force. She doesn't have to chase respect; she commands it by the way she values her own existence. When your vessel is full, your nurturing becomes a choice, not a chore. You give from your overflow, not from your marrow.

This is the ultimate goal of the "shoulders-high" lifestyle: to reach a point where your self-prioritization is so settled that you no longer have to explain it. You simply live it, and the world has no choice but to adjust to the new, protected reality of who you are.

This is the framework for choosing yourself without guilt. It is the realization that you are the primary steward of your life. If you don't protect your well-being, no one else will. You are not a martyr, and you are not a sacrifice. You are a woman of substance, a sanctuary in your own right, and you have every right to decide who is worthy of entering your gates. By setting these boundaries, you aren't being "too much"; you are finally being enough for yourself. And once you are enough for yourself, the world's attempts to make you "less" will finally lose their power. You walk with your shoulders high because you are finally standing on ground that you have reclaimed, and that ground is non-negotiable.

To truly understand how this perimeter is built, we have to look at the specific intersections where the theory of self-prioritization meets the messy, loud reality of cultural expectation. It is easy to talk about boundaries when you are alone in a room, but it is another thing entirely to hold that boundary when a family member is looking you in the eye and weaponizing your shared history against you. In the culture I was raised in, the "just manage" mentality is the default setting for family dysfunction. You are expected to be the shock absorber for a relative's bad choices simply because you share a surname.

I reached a point where I realized that my mental health was not a sacrifice I was willing to make on the altar of family loyalty. I had to face the reality that "blood is blood" is often the phrase used to keep you bleeding so that others can feel full.

I remember a specific period where the weight of this expectation felt physical. I had a family member who viewed my life as a communal resource. To them, my progress was not something to be celebrated, but something to be harvested. They didn't see me as a person with my own needs; they saw me as a financial safety net and an emotional bank. When I finally found the courage to say "no", when I refused to fund a crisis they had repeatedly manufactured for themselves, the reaction was swift. I wasn't met with a conversation; I was met with a smear campaign. This is the part of the journey that no one tells you about. When you stop being "useful," you quickly become the "villain." They will tell the rest of the family that you have changed, that you are arrogant, and that you have "forgotten where you came from."

This is the moment where most women fold. The fear of being the "bad person" in the family narrative is so strong that we would rather sacrifice our peace than deal with the noise of their disapproval. But I stayed settled in my choice. I realized that if the price of being "good" was my own depletion, then I was perfectly fine with being the antagonist in their story. I had to learn that their version of "me" was none of my business. When you are a woman of high standards, you realize that you cannot control the perception of people who benefit from your lack of boundaries. Their anger is just proof that the boundary was necessary. If they loved you for who you were, they would respect your limits. If they only loved you for what you gave, then their opinion of you was never based on the truth to begin with.

The Strategy of the Clean Exit

THE SELF-POSSESSED SHIELD

When you decide to remove access, you must do it with the same precision we've discussed in every other chapter. You do not need to have a big talk or a dramatic confrontation. In fact, a dramatic exit is often just another way of staying entangled; it's a performance that invites a rebuttal. True distance is not loud. It is the slow, deliberate withdrawal of your energy. It is the choice to stop answering the phone at 11:00 PM when you know the caller only wants to dump their chaos into your night. It is the refusal to engage in the guilt-tripping text thread that begins with "after all I did for you." True luxury in behavior is knowing that you don't owe anyone an explanation for why you are protecting your own peace.

The language you use in these moments must be final. If you provide a reason, you provide a target for them to hit. If you explain that you are too busy, they will try to fix your schedule. If you say you don't have the money, they will ask you to borrow it for them. But if you simply provide a result, I won't be able to do that; you are maintaining your containment. You are not asking for permission to have a limit; you are simply stating that the limit exists. This creates a psychological barrier that is very hard for a boundary violator to scale. It moves you from a state of negotiation to a state of declaration. It feels cold at first, but it is actually the highest form of self-respect. You are treating your life as a sanctuary that requires a specific protocol for entry.

You will be labeled, and you must make peace with that now. You will be called proud by people who used to walk all over you. You will be called too foreign by people who thrive on hardness and the "suffer-head" mentality. In many circles, a woman who prioritizes her rest and her grooming is seen as an insult to those who pride themselves on being disheveled and exhausted. They will say you are acting like a white person or that you have forgotten your roots because you no longer participate in the communal trauma. Let them speak. Their words are just noise outside the sanctuary you have built. If you are living a life where your cup is full, and your spirit is settled, their labels cannot stick to you. You aren't being proud; you are being prioritized. You aren't being foreign; you are being free.

The most difficult part of this journey is the mourning process that follows when you remove access from someone you still love. This is a specific kind of grief because the person is still there, but the relationship as you knew it is dead. You have to mourn the relationship you wish you had while acknowledging the reality of the one you actually have. This is the ultimate shoulders-high act: being honest about the fact that love is not enough to sustain a relationship that is killing you. You can love someone from the other side of a very high wall. You can wish them the very best in life while ensuring that their life never intersects with yours again. This isn't coldness; it is clarity. It is the realization that you cannot heal in the same environment that made you sick.

Life after a necessary exit is often characterized by a profound, startling silence. I remember walking away from a long-term friendship that had become a one-way street of emotional labor. For years, I had been the strong friend, the one who listened, the one who fixed, and the one who supported, while my own needs were treated like an annoying footnote. When I finally created distance, I expected to feel a massive sense of loss. Instead, I felt a massive sense of relief. It was as if I had been carrying a heavy rucksack for years and had finally set it

THE SELF-POSSESSED SHIELD

down. My aura changed because I was no longer on high alert, waiting for the next crisis to manage. My tone became more settled because I wasn't constantly defending my space. This is the life after that the world doesn't want you to see: the freedom to exist without the weight of someone else's unmanaged chaos.

In this new space, you find that your energy is finally your own. You no longer wake up wondering who is going to drain you today. You begin to see what your life looks like when it isn't a reaction to someone else's dysfunction. You find that you have more energy for your own grooming, your own rest, and the people who actually respect your perimeter. You realize that you were never a bad person for wanting peace; you were just in a situation that required you to be a martyr to be loved. Once you stop being a martyr, you can finally start being a woman. You can finally exude that magnetic, feminine confidence that only comes from someone who is truly her own primary concern.

Filling your own cup first is not about being anti-social; it is about being pro-soul. It is about recognizing that your presence is the most valuable thing you own. If you allow everyone to take a piece of you, there will eventually be nothing left for you to inhabit. By setting these boundaries, you are ensuring that the version of you that interacts with the world is the highest-quality version. You are moving from a place of forced service to a place of chosen contribution. This is the only way to live with the shoulders high. You build the wall, you set the protocol, and you mourn the ones who couldn't respect it. And then, you turn back to your own life, and you live it with a level of excellence that was impossible when you were busy carrying everyone else's bags.

CHAPTER 9
The Self-possessed Shield in Practice

When you look at the life you have been living up until this point, you might see a pattern of constant negotiation. This is the fundamental problem that most women face: we are taught to bargain away our peace just to keep everyone else comfortable. We have been conditioned to believe that if we are not being flexible, we are being difficult. This creates a life where you are always on edge, always checking the room to see if you are allowed to be yourself. You might find that you are constantly shrinking your needs to fit into the spaces people have carved out for you. This is the high cost of living without a perimeter. It is the exhaustion that comes from being a woman who is always available but never truly honored. You are tired because you have been trying to build a high-quality life on a foundation of compromise, and it simply does not work. You have spent years being the person who makes things easy for everyone else, while your own life feels harder and harder to manage every single day.

The problem starts when you realize that your kindness has become a weakness that people exploit. You find yourself saying yes to things that make your stomach churn because you are afraid of the friction that a no might cause. You tolerate the late friend who never apologizes, the dismissive partner who ignores your feelings, or the entitled relative who only calls when they want money.

You do this because you have been told that a good woman is one who manages the mess without complaining. But this constant management is exactly what is draining your light. You are trying to exude feminine energy while your nervous system is in a state of high alert, waiting for the next person to take a piece of you. You cannot be settled when you are constantly worried about when the next boundary violation is going to happen. You are living in a state of reaction rather than intention, and that is why you feel like you are losing your grip on who you actually are.

The Exhaustion of the Open Gate

The most visible part of this problem is the way people handle your time and your energy as if it belongs to them. When you do not have a self-possessed shield, you are like a house with no doors and no windows. Anyone can walk in at any time, leave their trash, and walk out whenever they feel like it. You find that you are the one people call when they need a favor, a ride, or a shoulder to cry on, but you are the last person they think of when they have something to celebrate.

You are the emotional dumping ground for everyone's drama, yet your own struggles are treated like an annoying footnote. This is not because people are inherently bad, but because you have trained them to treat you this way by never showing them where you end and where they begin. By constantly negotiating down your standards, you have signaled to the world that your time is cheap and your peace is not a priority.

THE SELF-POSSESSED SHIELD

This creates a cycle of resentment that is very hard to break once it starts. You start to feel bitter toward the people you love, not because of what they are doing, but because of what you are allowing them to get away with. You feel trapped by your own reputation for being nice. You want to walk with your shoulders high, but you feel heavy because you are carrying the weight of everyone else's expectations on your back. This is the reality of life without the self-possessed shield. It is a life of desperation where you are performing a version of yourself that is serviceable to others but completely empty for you. You are waiting for someone to come along and give you permission to stop being everyone's savior, but that permission is never going to come from the outside. You have to be the one to realize that the gate is open and that you are the only one who can close it.

We also have to talk about the physical toll of this problem. When you are always negotiating your worth, your body stays in a state of tension. Your shoulders stay up by your ears because you are braced for the next demand. Your voice stays high and fast because you are trying to be as unthreatening as possible.

Your grooming starts to slip because you feel like there is no point in putting in the effort if you are just going to be exhausted anyway. You begin to look as tired as you feel. This is a dangerous place to be because your physical state starts to confirm the lie that you are a low-value resource. When you look and act depleted, people treat you as if you are disposable. This is how the cycle of mediocrity continues, trapping you in a version of life that is far below what you are capable of experiencing.

The final layer of the problem is the fear of being alone. Many women stay in the negotiation phase because they are afraid that if they set a real boundary, everyone will leave. They are afraid that if they stop being the person who does everything for everyone, they will no longer be loved. This fear is what keeps the gate open. It is what makes you accept the "just manage" culture in your family and your friendships.

THE SELF-POSSESSED SHIELD

But you have to ask yourself: if these people only love you because you are a convenient tool, is that really love? If the price of their presence is your own self-destruction, is it worth paying? Living without a self-possessed shield means you are surrounded by people, but you have never felt more alone, because nobody is actually seeing or respecting the real you. They are only seeing the version of you that they can use.

- Reclaiming the Standard of One

The first solution to this problem is the total synthesis of your standards into a single way of being. You have to stop viewing your confidence, your grooming, and your boundaries as separate things you do depending on who is watching. Instead, you must allow them to merge into one unshakeable identity. This is where the self-possessed shield begins to take shape. It is the moment you decide that you are the standard of one. You no longer look to the room to see how you should behave or what level of respect you should settle for; you bring the behavior and the requirement for respect into the room with you. This means that your level of grooming stays high whether you are at a

THE SELF-POSSESSED SHIELD

five-star hotel or a local pharmacy. Your tone stays settled whether you are talking to a CEO or a clerk. Your boundaries stay firm whether you are dealing with a stranger or your own mother.

When you become the standard of one, you remove the need for external validation entirely. You stop asking, "Is this too much?" and you start knowing that it is exactly what you need. This creates a massive shift in how people perceive you almost instantly. When you are no longer looking for a green light to be excellent, people stop trying to give you a red light. Your self-possession acts as a natural filter for the people around you. It tells the world that you are a woman who is fully contained within herself and her own values. You are not looking for someone to fill your cup or tell you that you are doing a good job; you are already operating from a place of overflow. This makes you magnetic to high-value people, but it also makes you safe from those who want to use you. Because you are the one in charge of your energy, you no longer have to be afraid of being depleted by the world's noise.

THE SELF-POSSESSED SHIELD

This solution requires you to be very disciplined about your daily rituals, even when it feels difficult. Your shield is only as strong as the habits that support it every single day. This means your morning solitude is not a luxury you have when you have time; it is a requirement for your survival as a self-possessed woman. Your grooming routine is not about vanity or trying to impress others; it is about self-honor and showing yourself that you are worth the effort.

Your early nights and your weekends are not about being boring or antisocial; they are about protecting the resource that is your physical and mental health. When you treat your daily habits with this level of respect, the self-possessed shield becomes unshakeable. It is no longer something you have to "remember" to do; it is simply who you are. You move through the world with a firm presence that needs no explanation and no apology.

We also have to look at how this solution changes your communication. When you are the standard of one, you stop using the language of negotiation. You stop saying "if you don't mind" or "I'm sorry to bother you." You start using

THE SELF-POSSESSED SHIELD

direct, clear, and settled language. You state your needs as facts rather than requests. For example, instead of saying, "Could you please try to be on time next time?" you say, "I value my time, so I won't be able to wait more than fifteen minutes."

This shift in language is a key part of the solution because it reinforces your shield. It shows people that you are not looking for a compromise on your basic requirements. You are simply stating the terms of your presence. This might feel uncomfortable at first, but it is the only way to train the world to treat you with the precision you deserve.

The final part of this first solution is learning to be okay with being misunderstood. When you start living by the standard of one, people who used to benefit from your flexibility will be upset. They will call you difficult, proud, or stiff. This is where your confidence must act as the core of your shield. You have to realize that their misunderstanding of you is not your problem to fix. You don't need to explain why you have changed or why you are suddenly so particular about your time and space. You just have to

THE SELF-POSSESSED SHIELD

keep living your truth. Eventually, the people who actually belong in your life will adjust to the new standard, and the ones who don't will simply fall away. This is a good thing. It clears the field so that you can fill it with relationships that are built on mutual respect rather than one-sided sacrifice.

By implementing this solution, you are moving from a state of forced service to a state of chosen contribution. You are no longer giving because you feel you have to, but because you want to, from your own overflow. This is the only way to live with your shoulders high for the rest of your life. You build the shield by making small, consistent choices that honor your soul. You choose the restful night over the draining party. You choose the honest "no" over the lying "yes." You choose the polished appearance over the disheveled one. Each of these choices is a brick in the wall of your self-possessed shield. And as the wall gets higher and stronger, you will find that you are finally free to be the woman you were always meant to be; graceful, powerful, and completely her own.

Building on the idea of being the standard of one, we have to look at the next phase of this transformation. Once you have identified the problem of constant negotiation and accepted the first solution of setting your own internal rules, you must face the reality of the social friction that follows. The second solution is the mastery of the tactical pause and the implementation of the silent withdrawal.

This is how you handle the world when it tries to test your new shield. It is one thing to decide in the morning that you are a woman of high value; it is another thing to maintain that belief when you are standing in a budget space being treated like an afterthought, or when a loved one is pushing against your boundaries. This part of the process is where the self-possessed shield becomes a practical tool that handles the heat of the real world so that your spirit doesn't have to.

THE SELF-POSSESSED SHIELD

The tactical pause is the simplest yet most powerful tool in your possession. When the world demands something from you, a favor, an answer, or a reaction, most women feel a frantic need to respond immediately. This is the reflex of a woman who is still trying to be nice and serviceable. But a woman with a self-possessed shield understands the power of the gap. When someone asks you for something that feels like a drain on your energy, you don't answer right away. You pause. You take a breath. You let the silence sit in the air for a few seconds.

This pause does two things: it gives you time to check in with your own capacity, and it signals to the other person that your time and energy are not a fast-food transaction. It shows that you are a woman who thinks before she acts. This small moment of stillness is a key part of your shield because it prevents you from making promises you will later regret and keeps your frequency settled and in control.

- The Art of the Silent Withdrawal

The second solution is learning the art of the silent withdrawal. There is a common misconception that setting boundaries requires a lot of noise and confrontation. We think we have to sit people down for "the talk" or send long, emotional paragraphs explaining why we are upset. But the truth is that a self-possessed woman rarely needs to make a scene. She understands that her presence is her greatest bargaining chip, and the most effective way to use it is to withdraw it when the environment is no longer serving her. If you are in a social setting where the conversation has turned to gossip or negativity, you don't have to stay and "just manage" it. You don't even have to correct them. You simply and politely excuse yourself. You withdraw your light from the room. This applies to your relationships and your daily errands just as much as it does to your social life. If you are in a shop where the service is dismissive or the atmosphere is chaotic, you don't have to argue for better treatment. Arguing is a form of negotiation, and we have already decided that the negotiation phase is over. Instead, you simply leave. You take your business and your energy elsewhere.

THE SELF-POSSESSED SHIELD

In your personal life, if a relative is being toxic or a friend is being draining, you don't need a dramatic breakup. You just become less available. You stop being the first person to call. You stop being the one who always fixes the mess. This silent withdrawal is the most sophisticated form of self-defense. It doesn't leave any "hooks" for people to grab onto, and it keeps your energy contained. You aren't attacking them; you are simply prioritizing the health of your own perimeter.

By practicing the silent withdrawal, you are teaching people that access to you is a privilege, not a right. When people realize that you will simply walk away, not out of anger, but out of self-respect, they start to treat you differently. They realize that they cannot take your presence for granted. This solution is particularly effective in a "just manage" culture because it bypasses the typical cycles of guilt and drama.

THE SELF-POSSESSED SHIELD

You aren't fighting the culture; you are simply choosing not to participate in it. You are moving through the world like a woman who knows her worth is non-negotiable, and if a space cannot accommodate that worth, then that space is not for her. This is how you maintain your femininity; you don't have to get hard or mean because you are never in the room long enough for the toxicity to reach you.

This second solution also includes the discipline of protecting your "recovery time." A self-possessed shield requires a lot of fuel to stay operational, and that fuel comes from your rest. You must become a person who treats her sleep, her grooming rituals, and her solitude as sacred. If you are constantly on, constantly helping, and constantly available, your shield will inevitably become porous. You will start to make mistakes. You will start to say "yes" when you mean "no." Protecting your recovery time is the act of ensuring that your vessel is always full so that you never have to give from your marrow. It means being okay with saying, "I'm staying in tonight to rest," even when there is an "important" event. You realize that the most important event in your life is the maintenance of your own soul.

Living Within the Sanctuary

As we bring these pieces together, it is important to know that the self-possessed shield is not a destination you reach, but a way of moving through the world for the rest of your life. It is the realization that you are the primary steward of the life God gave you, and you have every right to protect it. You have moved from the problem of being a public utility to the solution of being a private sanctuary.

You have learned that your energy is a premium resource, your time is a finite gift, and your peace is the foundation of your power. This journey has not been about becoming someone else; it has been about stripping away the layers of social conditioning that told you that you were only valuable when you were being useful to others.

The final shift happens when you realize that you no longer need anyone else to understand why you live the way you do. You have reached a level of internal stabilization where the world's labels–proud, difficult, too much–no longer have any weight. You understand that those labels are just the noise made by people who are uncomfortable with a woman they cannot control.

You have chosen to be your own luxury, and in doing so, you have found a level of freedom that most women never experience. You walk with your shoulders high, not because you are trying to prove a point, but because you are finally standing at your full height. You are no longer shrinking, and you are no longer apologizing for the space you take up.

As you move forward from this book, I want you to carry this shield with you into every corner of your existence. Let it be the filter through which you view every invitation, every conversation, and every relationship. Remember that you are the lady of your own house, and you hold the keys to the gate. You have permission to be excellent. You have permission to be particular. You have permission to live a life that is beautiful, settled, and completely yours. The world will try to pull you back into the old cycles, but you now have the tools to stay firm. You have the energy of a queen, the confidence

THE SELF-POSSESSED SHIELD

of a woman who knows her worth, and the boundaries of a sanctuary.

This is the end of the "just manage" era of your life. From this moment on, you are a woman of the self-possessed shield. You move with grace, you speak with clarity, and you live with intention. You are no longer waiting for life to happen to you; you are the one who is happening to life. You have cleared the field, you have built the perimeter, and you have finally, beautifully, claimed your throne. So, take a deep breath, settle your shoulders, and walk out into the world. It is waiting for the woman you have finally decided to be. You are the standard. You are the premium. You are finally, unshakeably, yourself.

About the Author

Kele Chi Key writes for women who are ready to take charge of their lives.

Her work centers on a simple but often resisted truth: women are not meant to live depleted, overextended, or endlessly accommodating at the expense of their own well-being. Through her writing, she challenges the belief that sacrifice is the highest form of womanhood and invites women to place themselves back at the center of their own lives.

Kele Chi Key's philosophy is rooted in intentional living, disciplined self-respect, and embodied femininity. She believes that energy is a form of currency, peace is a non-negotiable standard, and boundaries are not acts of defiance but acts of self-leadership. In a world that often rewards self-abandonment, her work encourages women to become selective, discerning, and unapologetic about how they live, love, and give.

Her writing speaks to women who are willing to question inherited cultural norms and societal expectations, especially those that taught them to endure silently, explain endlessly, or earn rest through over-giving. She affirms that it is not only acceptable, but necessary, to remove people, patterns, and environments that deplete one's energy, compromise health, or disturb inner stability.

Kele Chi Key writes for the woman who is prepared to become her best self for herself first. The woman who understands that loving herself at the highest level allows her to show up more fully, intentionally, and sustainably for the people and purposes that truly deserve her presence. The woman who is comfortable being seen as difficult, selective, or unconventional when doing so protects her future and preserves her well-being.

This book is an extension of that philosophy, a guide for women ready to live with intention, exude femininity with structure and standards, and lead their lives from a place of self-respect rather than obligation.

www.ingramcontent.com/pod-product-compliance
Lightning Source LLC
Chambersburg PA
CBHW052129030426
42337CB00028B/5082